An
Anti-Capitalist
Manifesto

To Sam,
with love.

An Anti-Capitalist Manifesto

— Alex Callinicos —

polity

First published in 2003 by Polity Press in association with Blackwell Publishing Ltd

Editorial office:
Polity Press
65 Bridge Street
Cambridge CB2 1UR, UK

Marketing and production:
Blackwell Publishing Ltd
108 Cowley Road
Oxford OX4 1JF, UK

Distributed in the USA by
Blackwell Publishing Inc.
350 Main Street
Malden, MA 02148, USA

A catalogue record for this book is available from the British Library.

Library of Congress Cataloging-in-Publication Data

Callinicos, Alex.
An anti-capitalist manifesto / Alex Callinicos.
    p.   cm.
Includes bibliographical references and index.
ISBN 0-7456-2903-2 (hardbound : alk. paper) – ISBN 0-7456-2904-0 (pbk. : alk. paper)
1. Capitalism.   2. Radical economics.   3. Globalization.   4. Protest movements.   I. Title.
HB501 .C233 2003
330.12'2 – dc21

                                                                    2002009839

Typeset in 11 on 13 pt Sabon by SNP Best-set Typesetter Ltd., Hong Kong
Printed in Great Britain by MPG Books Ltd, Bodmin, Cornwell

This book is printed on acid-free paper.

Contents

Preface

This book was conceived and written on the run, between counter-summits and mobilizations. I drafted the final plan for the book in the departure lounge of Porto Alegre airport after the second World Social Forum, and wrote it in the midst of the preparations for the first European Social Forum in Florence. In retrospect, this book can be seen as forming the concluding part of a trilogy that began with *Equality* (1999) and continued with *Against the Third Way* (2001). Though they weren't planned like this, the three books can be thought of as a Hegelian triad, with *Equality* exploring universal principles of justice in the abstract, *Against the Third Way* representing the negative moment of critique, and *An Anti-Capitalist Manifesto* analysing the concrete movements that are now struggling to realize these principles by bringing into being a different world. Alternatively, and perhaps less pretentiously, this book can be read in its own right, as an argument about the nature of the international movement against capitalist globalization and the kind of strategy and programme it should pursue.

An Anti-Capitalist Manifesto reflects the contributions, direct and indirect, of many other activists and intellectuals in this movement. In the dialogue that is developing within the European radical left I have benefited especially from my contacts with Daniel Bensaïd, whose writings have become an important reference point. Mike Gonzalez accompanied me to Porto Alegre II, and I gained much from our discussions there. Chris Bambery, Chris Harman, Chris Nineham, and an anonymous referee read the manuscript in draft: I would like to thank them all for their advice and encouragement. Working with Polity has been, as usual, a pleasure: I am grateful in particular to Helen Gray, David Held, Rachel Kerr, and Pam Thomas. But my biggest debt is to Sam Ashman: she shared in many of the experiences that lie behind the book, read and commented on it in draft, and was a constant source of ideas and references. As justice commands, I have dedicated *An Anti-Capitalist Manifesto* to her.

Acknowledgements

The author and publishers would like to thank the following for permission to use copyrighted material:

The *Financial Times* for four extracts (pages 5–6, 40–1, 42–3 and 73) all © the *Financial Times*; The *Guardian* for two extracts (pages 19 and 63); Naomi Klein for an extract from 'The Vision Thing' published in *The Nation*, 10.7.2000, pp. 18–21, and from 'Masochistic Capitalists' published in the *Guardian*, 15.2.2002.

Every effort has been made to trace the copyright holders, but if any have been inadvertently overlooked, the publishers will be pleased to make the necessary arrangements at the first opportunity.

Introduction

An unscheduled event

Something strange happened at the end of the 1990s. Liberal capitalism had emerged triumphant from the collapse of the Communist regimes a decade earlier. Francis Fukuyama famously announced at the time that this development represented the End of History: the failure of Communism had shown that no progressive systemic alternative to liberal capitalism was feasible.[1] Few people bought the strange cocktail of neo-Hegelian philosophy and Reaganite triumphalism that informed Fukuyama's argument. But many accepted its substance. After all, postmodernism and its progeny (postcolonial theory, for example), deeply entrenched in the liberal English-speaking academy, had long before proclaimed the 'collapse of grand narratives' and the coming of a fragmented, plural world where the very idea of challenging liberal capitalism would threaten to revive the totalitarianism responsible for Auschwitz and the Gulag Archipelago.[2]

Much more important, the same general outlook has been reflected in public policy as well. In 1990 the economist John Williamson coined the expression 'Washington Consensus' to refer to no less than ten policy-areas in which decision-makers worldwide accepted a neo-liberal agenda – fiscal discipline, public expenditure priorities, tax reform, financial liberalization, competitive exchange-rates, trade liberalization, foreign direct investment, privatization, deregulation, and property rights.[3] During the Long Boom of the 1950s and 1960s, most of these policies would have been dismissed as the fantasies of economic heretics dreaming of a return to the nineteenth century: the mainstream view embodied some version or other of Maynard Keynes's claim that the stability of capitalism depended on state intervention to secure full employment. Susan George is therefore only exaggerating slightly when she writes: 'In 1945 or 1950, if you had seriously proposed any of the ideas and policies in today's standard neo-liberal toolkit you would have been laughed off the stage or sent to the insane asylum.'[4]

It was the first great post-war slump in the mid-1970s that created a more receptive climate for these heresies. Neo-liberalism nevertheless replaced Keynesianism as the economic orthodoxy as a result of major political and ideological struggles. During the 1980s Ronald Reagan in the United States and Margaret Thatcher in Britain successfully pioneered free-market policies, overcoming the resistance both of parts of the establishment and of powerful groups of workers such as the American air traffic controllers in 1981 and the British miners in 1984–5. By the end of that decade the world scene had become highly favourable to the generalization of these innovations. On the one hand, the debt crisis inherited from the second major economic slump at the beginning of the 1980s gave the International Monetary Fund and the World Bank the leverage they needed to force Third World governments to accept neo-liberal programmes of 'structural adjustment'; on the other hand, the collapse of Communism enabled the United States in particular to encourage the successor regimes in Central and Eastern Europe and the former

Soviet Union to undergo 'shock therapy' that dragged their economies abruptly from state controlled autarky to incorporation in a highly competitive world market.[5]

At a global level, the imposition of neo-liberal orthodoxy at least in part reflected a conscious strategy pursued by successful American administrations in order to maintain US hegemony in the post-Cold War era: the very name attached to these policies – the Washington Consensus – is symptomatic of the role played in their implementation by the institutional complex binding together the US Treasury, the IMF, and the World Bank.[6] But the triumph of these ideas was underlined by their acceptance by a wide section of the international left. The Third Way originated as a slogan intended to differentiate Bill Clinton's New Democrats from both Reaganite Republicanism and the statist approach to economic and social problems represented by earlier Democratic presidents such as Franklin Roosevelt and Lyndon Johnson. In fact, the Clinton administration's commitment to the neo-liberal agenda was soon confirmed by its strenuous and successful efforts, in close alliance with big business and the Republican right, to persuade the Congress to approve the North American Free Trade Agreement (NAFTA) in 1993.[7]

Preached with missionary zeal by Tony Blair and his court philosopher Anthony Giddens, the Third Way demanded an acceptance of what was represented as economic necessity. Globalization had rendered old left remedies such as redistribution and public ownership obsolete; the rebranded 'centre-left' had to embrace neo-liberal economics and authoritarian social policies prettified with some communitarian rhetoric.[8] The effect was, so to speak, to take the politics out of politics: given that everyone who mattered accepted liberal capitalism, political debate could only centre around minor technical issues and the presentation of personality. No wonder that Tony Blair flourished in this climate: the effects of his domination of British politics were evident in the numbingly tedious general election of June 2001. The absence of significant differences between the two mainstream candidates was an important factor in Jean Marie Le Pen's surprise success in the first round of the French presidential elections in April 2002, when he beat the Prime Minister, Lionel Jospin, into third place. It seemed as if the end of ideology, announced somewhat prematurely by Daniel Bell at the beginning of the 1960s, had finally arrived. Or rather – one ideology had definitively supplanted the rest. Perry Anderson, one of the key intellectuals of the Western left for the past generation, wrote: 'For the first time since the Reformation, there are no longer any significant oppositions – that is, systematic rival outlooks – within the thought-world of the West; and scarcely any on a world scale either, if we discount religious doctrines as largely inoperative archaisms.'[9]

By the time this sentence appeared in early 2000, it had become obsolete. For something untoward happened in Seattle at the end of November 1999. The World Trade Organization had gathered there to launch a new round of trade talks. High on the agenda was the liberalization of trade in services: the investment banks and multinational corporations, who had already done so well out of privatization, were greedily eyeing up the many public services that had so far managed to survive. Where better to stage yet another triumph for the Washington Consensus than Seattle, capital of the New Economy, to whose perpetual glory mass choirs of professional economists and investment consultants were then singing arias? But some uninvited guests turned up – 40,000 demonstrators, drawn from a wide spectrum of constituencies that extended from core sections of American organized labour (teamsters, longshoremen, machinists, for example) to a plethora of non-governmental organizations and activist coalitions campaigning around issues such as the environment, fair trade, and Third World debt. The numbers and militancy of the protesters, and the innovative methods of organizing they used, took the authorities by surprise. The resulting disruption made it harder for Western governments (divided in particular by a series of disputes between the US and the European Union) to get their act together and encouraged the representatives of Third World states to stand up to the big powers' bullying. So the talks collapsed. The neo-liberal juggernaut had, temporarily at least, been halted.

Nor was Seattle just a flash in the pan. Neo-liberal commentators and some of the old left, taken by surprise, dismissed the demonstrators as a protectionist rabble.[10] But the success of the protest helped to give millions of people around the world the confidence also to challenge neo-liberalism. One symptom of globalization – however it should be interpreted – has been the proliferation of summits symbolized by a plethora of acronyms, G8, IMF, EU, APEC, FTAA . . . Protests mainly directed at these events spread like wildfire – Washington (16 April 2000), Millau (30 June 2000), Melbourne (11 September 2000), Prague (26 September 2000), Seoul (10 October 2000), Nice (6–7 December 2000), Washington again (20 January 2001), Quebec City (20–1 April 2001), Gothenburg (14–16 June 2001) . . . Running through these demonstrations was a rising arc of confrontation between the demonstrators and the police, culminating (to date) in the huge protests at the G8 summit in Genoa on 20–1 July 2001, when riot police used the destructive tactics of a small minority of demonstrators (the anarchist Black Bloc) to unleash an orgy of violence that led to the shooting of a local youth, Carlo Giuliani.

In the aftermath of Genoa, the *Financial Times* launched a series around the theme of 'Capitalism under Siege' to investigate the rise of what it called 'counter-capitalism'. This involved

tens of thousands of committed activists at the nexus of a global political movement embracing tens of millions of people.

Just over a decade after the fall of the Berlin Wall and the 'End of History' promised by Francis Fukuyama . . .

there is a growing sense that global capitalism is once again fighting to win the argument . . . The new wave of activism has coalesced around the simple idea that capitalism has gone too far. It is as much a mood as a movement, something counter-cultural. It is driven by the suspicion that companies, forced by the stock markets to strive for ever greater profits, are pillaging the environment, destroying lives and failing to enrich the poor as they promised. And it is fuelled by the fear that democracy has become powerless to stop them, as politicians are thought to be in the pockets of companies and international political institutions are slaves to a corporate agenda.[11]

The revival of social critique

If the neo-liberal hegemony began with the opening of the Berlin Wall on 9 November 1989, then it lasted barely ten years, to the first great demonstration in Seattle on 30 November 1999. The Washington Consensus continues to provide the framework for policy-making in virtually every state, but it is now intensely contested. Seattle did not mark the beginning of that contestation, though it did take it to a qualitatively new level. This book is not a history of the movement against global capitalism, but it may nevertheless be helpful to mention some of the factors that contributed to its emergence.

- NAFTA proved to be a pivotal development. Though resistance to the agreement was unsuccessful, it helped to bring the debate over globalization into focus. Consequently, as Mark Rupert puts it, 'the dominant liberal narrative of globalization is being contested within the US from at least two distinct positions. One might be described as the cosmopolitan and democratically-oriented left. The other I will refer to as the nationalistic far right.' The first of these positions – what Rupert calls a 'participatory stance of transnational political engagement' – informed the activist networks that constituted the left opposition to NAFTA and went on to organize the expanding resistance to the free-trade agenda that, after helping to precipitate the collapse in 1998 of talks on a Multilateral Agreement on Investments that was designed to make the world safe for the multinationals, rolled into the Seattle protests.[12]

- NAFTA was significant in another respect. Its coming into force on 1 January 1994 was the occasion of an armed uprising in the state of Chiapas in south-eastern Mexico. Subcommandante Marcos, leader of the Zapatista Army of National Liberation (EZLN) that launched the rising, denounced NAFTA, under which peasants' constitutional right of access to common lands had been abolished, as 'a death sentence to the indigenous ethnicities of Mexico'.[13] The connection thus established between the plight of Mexico's indigenous communities and neo-liberalism – which Marcos described as having launched 'the Fourth World War', in which globalization acted as 'the totalitarian extension of the logic of the finance markets to all aspects of life' – was a consistent theme of Zapatista propaganda.[14] The EZLN leaders' highly effective use of the media – and the Internet – made their cause one of the rallying points of the emerging global movement. In fact, the Chiapas campaign was simply one among many struggles in the South through which a sense of worldwide resistance to neo-liberalism gradually took shape. The Nigerian activist Ken Saro-Wiwa – executed by the Nigerian military regime in November 1995 for his campaign to defend the Ogoni people from the depredations of Shell – was another symbol of indigenous peoples' resistance to the tyranny of global capitalism.
- The new movement was also promoted by the development of what has come to be known as 'global governance' – not merely the expansion of formal institutions of intergovernmental cooperation such as

the United Nations, G8, and the EU, but also the transnational public sphere that began to emerge as a result of the rapid expansion of the NGOs. John Lloyd suggests that the encouragement given to the NGOs through their participation in official conferences such as the 1992 Rio summit on global warming helped to produce a backlash when governments showed no sign of seriously seeking to achieve the ambitious objectives adopted at events of this nature.[15] The spread of the NGOs helped to stimulate new activist coalitions that initially concentrated on remedying specific wrongs – for example, internationalist humanitarian activism (so-called '*sans frontièrisme*') in France, and the No Sweats movement against the exploitation of Third World labour on North American campuses.

- The scandal of Third World debt provided another focus of generalization. Campaigning movements such as Jubilee 2000 spread the net of activism much wider through their success in involving the churches and other organizations not normally known for their militancy. In retrospect, the large anti-debt demonstrations at the G8 summits at Birmingham in 1998 and Cologne in 1999 were harbingers of the more spectacular confrontations at Seattle and Genoa.[16]

- The East Asian financial and economic crisis of 1997–8 proved to be another pivotal event. Though it was seized on by defenders of the Washington Consensus as vindicating the superiority of the Anglo-American model over Asian 'crony capitalism', for many others it demonstrated the dangers of a deregulated world economy where huge flows of speculative capital could make or break countries overnight. The crisis itself, combined with the IMF 'rescues' which offered as a cure yet more neo-liberal measures, had important ideological consequences, as a group of establishment figures – the hedge fund impresario George Soros and the economists Joseph Stiglitz, Paul Krugman, and Jeffrey Sachs – emerged as forceful critics of the

Washington Consensus. Stiglitz's abrupt removal as World Bank chief economist on the eve of the Seattle protests contributed to a climate in which the legitimacy of the international financial institutions was increasingly contested.[17]

- Finally, large-scale resistance to neo-liberalism erupted in one of the G7 countries themselves – France. The mass public sector strikes of November–December 1995 derailed the conservative coalition's programme of free-market 'reforms' and contributed to a popular shift leftwards that brought the 'plural left' to office under Lionel Jospin in June 1997. Jospin proceeded (behind the covering fire provided by his socialist rhetoric) to privatize on a far larger scale than his right-wing predecessors. In opposition to his government, a new left developed around the monthly *Le Monde diplomatique* and the movement against international financial speculation ATTAC.[18] One expression of this process of radicalization came in the first round of the French presidential elections in April 2002: while Jospin was unexpectedly knocked out of the race, the candidates of the far left won over 10 per cent of the vote. The global orientation of this new left can be illustrated in various ways – in the emergence of the peasant leader José Bové as a symbol of resistance to genetically modified organisms and other threats to sound agricultural practice, in the role played by *Le Monde diplomatique* and ATTAC in the World Social Forums held in Porto Alegre, Brazil, and in ATTAC's international expansion (by the beginning of 2002 it had affiliates in forty countries).

This process of contestation involves more than activist campaigning and street protests. One reason why we can talk about a global *movement* is that it has found ideological articulation in a body of critical writing produced by a variety of intellectuals. They include two major figures. From the 1995 strikes till his death in January

2002, Pierre Bourdieu threw his immense prestige as a leading French intellectual into the struggle against neo-liberalism; with Raisons d'agir, a group of scholar-activists, he launched a series of short, cheap books including two volumes of polemical essays by Bourdieu himself, *Contre-feux* and *Contre-feux 2*. Noam Chomsky, for the past generation a lonely but consistent critic of American foreign policy, found himself reaching a worldwide audience that very readily followed his prompting to set the assertions of American imperial power he diagnosed in the context of the operations of global capitalism. Alongside these two grand figures of an older generation stood many others, already well-established writers and activists who now found a larger audience – for example, Michael Albert, Walden Bello, Susan George, and Toni Negri – and younger intellectuals who suddenly leapt into prominence, notably Naomi Klein and Michael Hardt. All the forementioned are authors of important books, but they are even more widely read thanks to the feverish circulation of texts via the Internet.

The emergence of this body of writing marked a wider shift in the intellectual constellation. In a massive study that is itself a contribution to the genre it analyses, Luc Boltanski and Eve Chapiello have documented what they call the 'renewal of social criticism' in France during the 1990s in reaction to the experience of neo-liberalism.[19] But social criticism was precisely the kind of discourse that postmodernism sought to prohibit. Jean Baudrillard, for example, writes: 'All our problems today as civilized beings originate here: not in an excess of alienation, but a disappearance of alienation in favour of a maximum transparency between subjects.'[20] The concept of alienation that provides the Marxist critique of capitalism with one of its main themes implies a contrast between an authentic subject and existing social relations that deny it self-realization. This contrast is, for example, implicit in the critique developed by the Situationists of 'the society of the spectacle' during the 1960s. For Guy Debord, modern capitalist societies were characterized by the dominance of the spectacle: 'Everything that was directly lived has moved away into a representation,' a state of affairs amounting to 'the concrete inversion of life'.[21]

But, as Boltanski and Chapiello observe, in this same period the concept of authenticity came under a series of formidable intellectual attacks by thinkers such as Gilles Deleuze and Jacques Derrida, whose work had a formative influence on postmodernism. Boltanski and Chapiello suggest that their deconstruction of the opposition between authenticity and inauthenticity contributed to the neo-liberal triumph in the 1980s and early 1990s: 'Much better in effect, from the standpoint of unlimited accumulation, that the question be suppressed, that people convince themselves that everything can no longer be anything but a simulacrum, that "true" authenticity is henceforth excluded from the world, or that the aspiration to the "authentic" is only an illusion.'[22] Baudrillard is the high priest of this deconstruction of authenticity, arguing that critical thought and political struggle had been rendered obsolete in a society, not of the spectacle but of simulation, where images no longer represent but now constitute reality.[23]

The re-emergence of anti-capitalist discourses and movements therefore marks the breakdown of the hegemony that postmodernism has exerted over avant-garde thinking over much of the past two decades. One sign of this intellectual shift is a decline in the almost obsessive concern with cultural questions that came to dominate the radical academy in the 1990s and a renewed preoccupation with the material. This is sometimes most marked among thinkers previously associated with postmodernism. Richard Rorty, whose writings played a crucial role in the reception of postmodernism into American intellectual culture, for example, has recently taken to criticizing what he calls 'the cultural left' in the US for its inattention to the growing divisions in American society caused by globalization.[24] The fact that Rorty himself helped to invent this cultural left and that his remedy – a return to social democracy – appears manifestly inadequate in no way alters the pertinence of his diagnosis.

Other instances could be given of this kind of reversal – one of the most striking has been the enthusiasm with which the Lacanian cultural theorist Slavoj Žižek has embraced Marx and even Lenin in recent years.[25] But the best example of the displacement of the cultural by a more traditional critique of capitalism is provided by the new movement's best-known text, Naomi Klein's *No Logo*. This book skilfully and wittily occupies the intellectual terrain beloved of a thousand Cultural Studies Departments schooled by Baudrillard – the thick description of contemporary trends in mass culture – only to lead its readers onto a new battlefield, by using the nuances of corporate branding to reveal the prevailing patterns of capitalist domination and the emerging forms of resistance. In the chapter where Klein documents how the preoccupation of her own generation of campus activists with identity politics and political correctness during the late 1980s and early 1990s actually dovetailed in with corporate strategies designed to extract value from multiculturalism we can hear an entire intellectual paradigm come crashing down in ruins:

And what is striking in retrospect is that in the very years when PC politics reached their most self-referential peak, the rest of the world was doing something very different: it was looking outward and expanding. At the moment when the field of vision among most left-wing progressives was shrinking to include only its immediate surroundings, the horizons of global business were expanding to encompass the whole globe . . . As we look back, it seems like wilful blindness. The abandonment of the radical economic foundations of the women's and civil-rights movements by the conflation of causes that came to be called political correctness successfully trained a generation of activists in the politics of image, not action. And if the space invaders marched into our schools and communities unchallenged, it was at least because the political models in vogue at the time of the invasion left many of us ill-equipped to deal with issues that were more about ownership than representation. We were too busy analysing the pictures being projected on the wall to notice that the wall itself had been sold.[26]

Naming the movement

And so the great debate over capitalism has been resumed, two hundred years after it began in the aftermath of the Great French Revolution. Postmodernism is now history. It is too well entrenched, particularly in the North American academy, simply to disappear, and so it will linger on, and perhaps even enjoy new leases of life among disciplines too parochial to have noticed its first assaults (there has been an especially risible vogue for postmodernism among English-speaking political science and international relations specialists in recent years). Nevertheless, the debate has moved on, less because of some decisive theoretical refutation of postmodernism (the most damaging philosophical critiques were produced during its heyday and seemed to have little effect on its influence) than because the worldwide rebellion against capitalist globalization has changed the intellectual agenda.

There is, however, one issue that causes some embarrassment. What should we call this new movement? The name usually applied to it – the anti-globalization movement – is plainly an absurd appellation for a movement that revels precisely in its international character and that has been able to mobilize highly effectively across national borders on all five continents. Leading figures in the movement have rightly distanced themselves from this name. Naomi Klein writes: 'it is not useful to use the language of anti-globalization.'[27] At the first World Social Forum at Porto Alegre in January 2001 Susan George said: 'we are "pro-globalization" for we are in favour of sharing friendship, culture, cooking, solidarity, wealth and resources.'[28] Vittorio Agnoletto of the Genoa Social Forum has expressed his dislike of the 'no-global' label by which the movement is known in Italy.[29]

Many North American activists are drawn to the distinction, apparently first made by Richard Falk, between two kinds of globalization – 'globalization-from-above, reflecting the collaboration between leading states and the main agents of capital formation', and 'globalization-from-below, . . . an array of transnational social forces animated by environmental concerns, human rights, hostility to patriarchy, and a vision of human community based on the unity of diverse cultures seeking an end to' poverty, oppression, humiliation, and collective violence.'[30] Others seek to qualify the kind of globalization they oppose differently, referring to 'corporate', or 'neo-liberal', or (very confusingly for English-speakers) 'liberal' globalization. This diverse usage reflects more than terminological differences. It has become a cliché to say that the movement of Seattle and Genoa is clearer about what it is against than what it is for. But this isn't really true: undeniably, the movement has left open both what its alternative to neo-liberalism is and how it intends to achieve it. But these ambiguities are related to a lack of clarity about who the enemy is. Crucially, is the enemy neo-liberalism – that is, the policies embodied in the Washington Consensus and the Anglo-American model of capitalism that these policies seek to universalize, or the capitalist mode of production itself? How one answers this question will help to determine the alternative one prefers and the strategy required to realize it.

In my view the movement is best described as anti-capitalist. This is not because a majority of activists think it possible or perhaps even desirable to replace capitalism altogether. The collapse of Communism still makes itself felt in the comparative weakness of the traditional left and in the lack of credibility of socialism as a systemic alternative to capitalism. Nevertheless, the movement is what Giovanni Arrighi, Terence Hopkins, and Immanuel Wallerstein would call an *anti-systemic* movement.[31] That is, it does not simply campaign over specific grievances or issues – say, to do with free trade or the environment or Third World debt – but is motivated by a sense of the interconnection between an immense variety of different injustices and dangers. Agnoletto has described his own political trajectory as representative of a movement from the specific to the general undergone by many other activists. Involved in the far-left Democrazia Proletaria in the 1970s, he drifted away and became, as a doctor, active in the AIDS movement in Italy during the 1980s and 1990s. When anti-retroviral drugs became widely available in the North during the mid-1990s, Agnoletto's attention shifted to the plight of HIV- and AIDS-sufferers in the Third World. Here he confronted the obstacle represented by the drug companies' assertion, backed up by the WTO, of their patent rights. So he found himself linking up with other NGOs to campaign against the WTO and, then, after Genoa, becoming one of the leaders of the Social Forums that have spread throughout Italy and become one of the main centres of the global movement.[32]

It is this developing consciousness of the system that, more than anything else, characterizes the movement. Already, at Seattle, Gerald McIntee, leader of the public sector union AFSCME, revived an old 1960s slogan: 'We have to name the system . . . and that system is corporate capitalism.'[33] The fact that a trade-union leader strongly committed to supporting the Clinton administration should have chosen to indulge in such radical rhetoric is a sign of the changing ideological climate. The anti-systemic focus of the movement is evident in its most important programmatic document to date, the Call of the Social Movements issued at the second World Social Forum in February 2002: 'We are building a large alliance from our struggles and resistance against a system based on sexism,

racism and violence, which privileges the interests of
capital and patriarchy over the needs and aspirations of
people.'[34]

Another unscheduled event

For some, however, this effort properly to characterize the
anti-capitalist movement is beside the point, since they
believe the movement itself has been overtaken by events.
The first part of the *Financial Times* series devoted to
'counter-capitalism' appeared on 11 September 2001. The
paper, which previously had followed the development of
the movement in great (and rather nervous) detail, noted
some weeks after 9–11: 'One of the less remarked consequences of the US terrorist attacks has been to halt in its
tracks the mass movement against globalization.'[35] Other
hostile commentators went further, seeking to smear the
movement by association with terrorism. According to
John Lloyd, a journalist close to New Labour,

> the anti-Americanism that develops into, or at least
> supports, terrorism presents a challenge to the anti-
> Americanism of some of the global movements. It plays on
> some of the same strings; and given that it is now so
> obvious that the stakes are very high, those who hold these
> views must make a careful accounting of how seriously
> they do so . . . The only political grouping now using the
> tactics developed by the global movements – sporadic use
> of violence and oppositionism through uncontrollable and
> unpredictable networks – is Bin Laden's al-Qaeda.[36]

This is pretty contemptible stuff. It equates a secret
network that regards the mass killing of airline passengers
and crew, office-workers, and fire-fighters as a legitimate
tactic with a movement that constantly affirms its commitment to open and democratic self-organization and to
peaceful protest. The violence that has been stupidly practised by the anarchist fringe in the Black Bloc at various

anti-capitalist protests is trivial stuff: trashing McDonald's or torching a few ATMs is hardly comparable to flying airliners into the World Trade Center. The only weapons fired at protests have been by police officers aiming at demonstrators. And to describe a movement whose most famous protest took place in the US as anti-American is just silly.

For all that, 9–11 did represent a blow to the anti-capitalist movement, particularly in North America. Protests scheduled for the IMF and World Bank annual general meetings in Washington at the end of September 2001 were cancelled. The WTO ministerial meeting, held the same November in Doha, capital of that stronghold of 'democratic governance' the Gulf sheikhdom of Qatar, succeeded in launching the round of trade negotiations blocked at Seattle. The Bush administration's declaration of a 'war on terrorism' and the associated curtailment of civil liberties, particularly in the US and Britain, created a much less hospitable climate for any form of protest (alarmingly, the FBI and other US law enforcement agencies have rediscovered the McCarthyite concept of 'unAmerican activities'). Some supporters of the anti-capitalist movement found reasons to support the war in Afghanistan, for example, entertaining what proved to be the illusion that overthrowing the Taliban would free Afghans – and in particular Afghan women – from the rule of intolerant Islamist warlords.[37] And – perhaps most seriously in the longer term – the slaughter on 9–11 of precisely the sort of white-collar and manual workers on whose support the long-term success of the anti-capitalist movement would depend threatened to destroy the so-called 'Teamster-Turtle alliance' – the coming together of organized labour and NGO activists – that had been such an important feature of Seattle and some later protests (notably those at Quebec City, Genoa, and Barcelona).

The effect of this setback was not, however, to destroy the movement, but rather to shift its centre of gravity from North America to Europe and Latin America. The demonstrations at Genoa in July 2001 marked the first stage of a process of radicalization that swept through Italian society, reviving the left after twenty years in the doldrums. The Genoa Social Forum that had organized the protests provided an organizational model for a nationwide movement in which diverse tendencies learned to work together constructively. This movement responded to the war in Afghanistan with a series of mass protests. In Britain, which had sent a major contingent to the Genoa protests, opposition to the 'war in terrorism' and to the Israeli reign of terror in the Occupied Territories brought into existence for the first time a movement comparable to those on the Continent and in North America: the large anti-war rallies and demonstrations were dominated by young activists – the people of Seattle and Genoa, so to speak.

But even these Italian and British movements were dwarfed by the giant protest 'Against a Europe of Capital and War' outside the EU summit in Barcelona on 16 March 2002. Organizers and authorities alike were taken by surprise as half a million mainly local people turned out on what the *Financial Times* called 'a peaceful demonstration against global capitalism, . . . underlining that their movement did not die with the September 11 attacks against the US and that their protests need not be marred by violence'.[38] Meanwhile, the second World Social Forum, which met in Porto Alegre at the beginning of February 2002, was three or four times the size of its predecessor. Between 65,000 and 80,000 activists, the large majority from Brazil itself, gathered to attend what amounted to a kind of world parliament of the anti-capitalist movement. The WSF resonated with an event further to the south – the mass rebellion against neo-liberalism that shook Argentina in December 2001. No longer could the movement be dismissed as an affair of the affluent North.

In some ways, 9–11 and the 'war on terrorism' – appalling and unwelcome developments though they were – produced a deepening of the anti-capitalist movement.

They forced activists to confront what Claude Serfati calls 'armed globalization' – the process through which capitalist globalization exacerbates existing geopolitical and social tensions and therefore demands the assertion of military power, above all by the US and its allies.[39] The Call of the Social Movements adopted at Porto Alegre II denounced 'the beginning of a permanent global war to cement the domination of the US government and its allies ... The opposition to war is at the heart of our movement.' Another sign of broadening horizons was the involvement of hundreds of anti-capitalist activists who participated in the efforts of the International Solidarity Movement to form human shields seeking to block access to the West Bank during the Israel Defence Force's brutal offensive against the Palestinian Authority in the spring of 2002. George Monbiot commented:

> The movement's arrival on the West Bank is an organic development of its activities elsewhere. For years it has been contesting the destructive foreign policies of the world's most powerful governments, and the corresponding failures of the multilateral institutions to contain them ... In Palestine, as elsewhere, it is seeking to place itself between power and those whom power affects.[40]

But if the anti-capitalist movement has both survived 9–11 and been prompted by the 'war on terrorism' to widen its focus, there remain very important questions that it must address. These, as I have already indicated, concern the nature of the enemy, the strategies required to overcome this enemy, and the alternative society that victory would bring into existence. It has in many ways been a source of strength that the movement has up to date been ambiguous in its responses to all these questions, but it does not follow that this will remain the case. The aim of this book is to offer one set of answers to these questions. Though it contains a programme (in chapter 3), it is less a political manifesto than an extended argument about

what the anti-capitalist movement should stand for. It
has been loosely inspired by Karl Marx's and Friedrich
Engels's *Manifesto of the Communist Party*. It would, of
course, be a foolish undertaking to attempt to improve on
or update such a classic. But the *Manifesto* is the most celebrated statement of Marx's critique of the capitalist mode
of production – a critique that the anti-capitalist movement is resuming in both theory and practice, even if most
of its activists would reject the label 'Marxist'. Marx is
therefore a major reference point in what follows, and I
have sporadically drawn on the *Manifesto*'s form.[41] Naturally this short book can make no claim to be definitive.
The anti-capitalist movement embraces a variety of different political perspectives and a commitment to unity in
diversity is one of its most strongly affirmed – and widely
practised – organizing principles. This is *an* anti-capitalist
manifesto: there can and should be many others. My
arguments represent one particular take on what this
movement is about – and one that is more influenced by
the revolutionary Marxist tradition than probably many
would find comfortable. I offer them all the same both as
a contribution to debate within the movement and in the
hope of persuading more people that another world is
indeed possible.

– 1 –

Capitalism Against the Planet

So what's the problem?

'Capitalism is clearly the best system for generating wealth, and free trade and open capital markets have brought unprecedented economic growth to most if not all of the world.'[1] This statement by Noreena Hertz, who has gone to some lengths to associate herself with the anti-capitalist movement, rather paradoxically sums up the neo-liberal case. Let us concentrate first on the latter part of the sentence. This asserts, as apologists for the World Bank and the IMF have endlessly claimed, that the liberalization of trade and investment of the past two decades has generated rapid economic growth; defenders of the Washington Consensus go on to argue that, thanks to this growth, global poverty and inequality can be reduced. Thus, shortly before the World Trade Organization meeting at Doha in November 2001 launched a new round of trade talks, the World Bank issued a report that estimated that abolishing all trade barriers could boost global income by $2,800 billion and lift 320 million people out of poverty.[2] A more vulgar form of the same kind of argument was provided by Clare Short, British Secretary of State for International Development, when she attacked the Seattle protestors, saying that the WTO was 'a precious international institution' and that 'those who make blanket criticisms of the WTO are working against, not for the interests of the poor and the powerless'.[3]

One could respond critically to this kind of claim in various ways. One can, for example, challenge the equation of human development with economic growth.[4] One can also point to the apparently relentless widening of global inequality that has occurred in the heyday of the Washington Consensus. According to research by Branko Mihailovic of the World Bank, by 1998 the income of the richest 1 per cent of the world's population equalled that of the poorest 57 per cent, while the global gini efficient (which measures the degree of inequality) had risen to 66.[5] It is, however, important to see that the neo-liberal argument can also be challenged in its own terms. The Center for Economic and Policy Research (CEPR) has undertaken a detailed comparison between the era of globalization (1980–2000) and the preceding two decades (1960–80), which saw Keynesian policies of demand management first achieve their apogee in the US under the Kennedy and Johnson administrations and then fall into disarray as a result of the economic crisis of the mid-1970s. The CEPR used several indicators – the growth of income per person, life expectancy, mortality among infants, children, and adults, literacy, and education – in order to compare performance in the two periods. It summarized the results of this comparison as follows:

> For economic growth and almost all the other indicators, the last 20 years have shown a very clear decline in progress as compared with the previous two decades. For each indicator, countries were divided into five roughly equal groups, according to what level the countries had achieved by the start of the period (1960 or 1980). Among the findings:

- *Growth: The fall in economic growth rates was most pronounced and across the board for all groups or countries.* The poorest group went from a per capita GDP growth of 1.9 per cent annually in 1960–1980, to a *decline* of 0.5 per cent per year (1980–2000). For the middle group (which includes mostly poor countries), there was a very sharp decline from an annual per capita growth rate of 3.6 per cent to just less than 1 per cent. Over a 20-year period, this represents the difference between doubling national income per person, versus increasing it by just 21 per cent. The other groups also showed substantial declines in growth rates.

- *Life Expectancy: Progress in life expectancy was also reduced* for 4 out of the 5 groups of countries, with the exception of the highest group (life expectancy 69–76 years). The sharpest slowdown was in the second to worst group (life expectancy between 44–53 years). Reduced progress in life expectancy and other health outcomes cannot be explained by the AIDS pandemic.

- *Infant and Child Mortality: Progress in reducing infant mortality was also considerably slower than during the period of globalization* (1980–1998) than over the previous two decades. The biggest declines in progress were for the middle to worst performing groups. Progress in reducing child mortality (under 5) was also slower for the middle to worst performing groups of countries.

- *Education and Literacy: Progress in education also slowed during the period of globalization.* The rate of growth of primary, secondary, and tertiary (post-secondary) school enrolment was slower for most groups of countries. There are some exceptions, but these tend to be concentrated among the better performing groups of countries. By almost every measure of education, including literacy rates, the middle and poorer performing groups saw less rapid progress in the period of globalization rather than in the prior two decades. The rate of growth of public spending in education, as a share of GDP, also slowed across all groups of countries.[6]

Annual growth rates by region 1961–98

Region	1961–80	1985–98
OECD	3.8	2.3
Latin America	5.1	3.2
Sub-Saharan Africa	4.2	2.1
East and South-East Asia	6.8	7.5
South Asia	3.6	5.6

Source: J. Weeks, 'Globalize, Globa-lize, Global Lies: Myths of the World Economy in the 1990s', in R. Albritton et al., eds, *Phases of Capitalist Development* (Houndmills, 2001)

These comparisons do not provide much support for the idea of trickle-down – that is, for the thought that faster economic growth would necessarily improve the plight of the poor. To the extent that there was improvement during what the CEPR paper calls 'the era of globalization', it occurred at a slower rate than in the 1960s and 1970s. But – even more striking – rates of output growth per head actually fell during a period when free-market orthodoxy would predict the opposite, since the liberalization of capital and product markets should (according to the theorems of neo-classical economics) have caused growth to accelerate. Moreover, as the authors point out, the comparison can hardly be described as loaded against the neo-liberal era, given that the earlier period encompassed the 1970s, which were marked by the first post-war slump and the beginnings of the second one. Other studies confirm the same picture: consider, for example, the table above, which compares growth-rates before and after the triumph of neo-liberalism.

John Weeks comments:

> the country groups that introduced the globalization poli-cies to the greatest degree fared least well in the 1990s relative to previous decades (the OECD, the Latin Ameri-can and the sub-Saharan countries); the best performing group since 1960, East and South-East Asia, entered into a severe recession in the 1990s; and the group whose

growth improved in the 1990s without recession, South Asia, was that which least adopted polic[i]es of deregulation, trade liberalization and decontrol of the capital account. The hypothesis that those policies foster growth is unconfirmed; that is, it is a myth of globalization.[7]

Behind such studies lies the larger fact that the world economy has yet to return to the growth rates it achieved during the Golden Age – what the French call *Les Trentes glorieuses*, the thirty glorious years – of the post-war boom, when trade and investment were considerably more regulated than they have been in the past two decades. Judged by its own yardstick of economic growth, then, neo-liberalism has been a failure. But, from the perspective of the Washington Consensus, the problem has arisen, not from too much privatization and deregulation, but too little. Hence, for example, the constant demands that the continental European and Japanese economies, both stagnant since the early 1990s, should adopt radical free-market 'reforms' that would allow them more closely to approximate the Anglo-American model of *laissez-faire* capitalism and thereby to achieve the dynamic growth that is supposedly a property of this model.

The same thinking led the IMF to demand that Argentina respond to the economic crisis that afflicted it as a result of the East Asian financial crash of 1997–8 with increasingly savage budget cuts. Joseph Stiglitz comments: 'Fiscal austerity was supposed to restore confidence. But the numbers in the IMF programme were fiction; any economist would have predicted that contractionary policies would incite slow-down, and that budget targets would not be met . . . Confidence is seldom restored as an economy goes into deep recession and double-digit unemployment.'[8] Even after these policies had precipitated financial collapse and an extraordinary rebellion of the unemployed and the middle class that brought down President Fernando de la Rúa in late December 2001, the IMF and the US Treasury continued to seek yet more budget cuts from his successor Eduardo Duhalde. The *Financial Times* brutally commented: 'Argentina can no longer afford its middle class. Economists calculate that real wages must fall 30 per cent for Argentina to compete with its peers around the world.'[9]

For increasing numbers of people, this is a crazy way to run the world. They see neo-liberalism not as the cure, but as the disease. But how deep does the problem lie? To some – Stiglitz is a distinguished example of this approach – the trouble comes, not from capitalism itself, but from a particular set of misguided policies being pursued by Western governments and the international financial institutions. Others offer a similar, if slightly more radical critique by saying that what's wrong is the prevailing model of capitalism. If only policies were adopted that permitted a return to the more regulated and humane capitalism of the post-war era, then most of the worst ills afflicting humankind could begin to be addressed.[10] A main thrust of this entire book is to challenge this kind of argument. It is capitalism itself and the logic that governs it – a logic of exploitation and competitive accumulation – that is the problem. Neo-liberalism, by stripping away many of the institutions and practices that made capitalism (at least in the prosperous North) bearable, has brought into sharper focus its constitutive defects, but these defects have always been there, and can only be removed, I believe, through its overthrow.

In the rest of this chapter, I begin to develop arguments supporting this conclusion (though it will take the entire book to complete my case). These concentrate in the first instance on the workings of capitalism as an economic system. This kind of economic analysis is essential to developing the anti-capitalist case. In the first place, capitalism is, first and foremost, an economic system – what Marx called a mode of production. Its defenders rely heavily on the claim that capitalism is superior to other social systems above all in its capacity to generate economic growth. Second, economics matters in the sense that individuals' opportunities to achieve the well-being and develop the capabilities that they have reason to value are heavily dependent on their access to productive resources. But the case against capitalism isn't solely an economic one. It is clear that one of the most powerful motivating forces behind the anti-capitalist movement is a rebellion against the process of commodification that has been accelerating since the neo-liberal hegemony was established.

'*Le Monde N'est Pas Une Marchandise!*' – 'The World Is Not For Sale!' – is one of the main slogans of the movement. It expresses opposition to the wholesale privatization of public assets and services that has spread like a cancer around the world, driven by an alliance of the institutions of the Washington Consensus, politicians who embrace neo-liberalism out of conviction or expediency, and investment banks, multinational corporations, and local businesses that stand to profit from the rundown of the state sector.[11] But this opposition tends to involve more than the belief that privatization has negative social and economic consequences, amply justified though that is by experiences such as the sell-off of Britain's railways. Informing it is a moral revulsion against the debasement produced by the reduction of everything to a commodity to be bought and sold. Of nowhere is this more true than in the cultural sphere. When Theodor Adorno and Max Horkheimer coined the expression 'the culture industry' they intended it as an ironical and critical concept: nothing seemed to them more absurd or contradictory than to reduce the creative processes to an industry governed by the same logic of rationalization as any other.[12] But in Britain today – in Europe at least the vanguard state of the neo-liberal coalition – cabinet ministers refer to the cultural industries without any sense of paradox or discomfort, and the *Financial Times* has a regular supplement called 'Creative Business'. The results of this direct subordination of cultural production to the priorities of profitable accumulation can be witnessed daily on television, where lust, greed, celebrity, and lifestyle fuse in a mutually reinforcing circuit of nightmarish banality. Nor is this merely a First World concern. For the Zapatista leader Marcos, for example, neo-liberalism is waging 'a planetary war' one of whose aims is 'a destruction of history and culture'.[13] One impulse behind the anti-capitalist movement is the desire to escape, to create a space free from the imperatives of the market.

Financial follies

But how large should this space be? To begin to answer this question we must begin to consider how deeply the trouble with capitalism goes. For many, the problem derives chiefly from the power that financial markets have acquired in recent years. Thus Walden Bello, Kamal Malhotra, Nicola Bullard, and Marco Mezzera write: 'The globalization of finance meant that increasingly its dynamics serve as the engine of the global capitalist system.'[14] The widespread perception, especially since the Asian and Russian crashes of 1997–8, that the dominance of the financial markets has greatly increased global economic instability provided one of the main stimuli behind the mushrooming movement, spearheaded by ATTAC (Association pour une taxation des transactions financières pour l'aide aux citoyens) in France and its affiliates elsewhere, demanding the introduction of the Tobin Tax on international currency transactions.[15]

Behind the asserted dominance of financial capitalism are a number of distinct, though interrelated phenomena:

- To begin with, there is the sheer size of globally integrated financial markets: Daily foreign exchange transactions rose from $800 billion in 1992, to $1200 billion in 1995, and nearly $1600 billion in 1998:[16] these astonishing figures reflect the fact that capital is much more internationally mobile than it was during the era of the Bretton Woods system after the Second World War;

- National governments have become much more vulnerable to the international bond-market where their debt is bought and sold: as John Grahl puts it, 'the globalized bond market is a sword of Damocles suspended over domestic policy-makers' heads', even in the most powerful states, as the Clinton administration discovered in 1993;[17]

- The increasing dominance of investment decisions by stock markets: this can be seen in a variety of ways, ranging from 'securitization' – the transformation of everything possible into a financial asset that can be bought, sold, and speculated in (the Enron energy trading empire developed, among other things, weather futures) – to the pressure on corporate executives to give overriding priority to 'shareholder value' – higher equity prices reflecting at least the prospect of dramatically improved profits, a development that has produced what Grahl calls 'a new balance of forces between proprietors and managers, very much in favour of the former';[18]

- The rapid growth of speculation in increasingly complex financial derivatives reflected in the rise of hedge funds that specialize in these assets, and whose activities can have enormous potential consequences for the world economy, as was shown by the spectacular collapse of the hedge fund Long-Term Capital Management at the height of the global financial panic following the Asian and Russian crashes in the autumn of 1998;

- The US boom of the late 1990s, which combined a genuine expansion of output and productivity (though whether and how far the rate of productivity growth increased is a matter of great controversy) with the development of a gigantic speculative bubble centred on Wall Street: hype and economic reality were hopelessly intermingled in the euphoric – and rapidly refuted – belief that the 'New Economy' represented America's liberation from the restraints of the business cycle.[19]

The financial markets are often represented as an autonomous, almost a natural phenomenon: thus television news programmes report the day's share prices along with the weather. Marx described capitalism as a 'bewitched, distorted, topsy-turvy world haunted by Monsieur le Capital and Madame la Terre, who are at the same time social characters and things'.[20] The representation of financial markets as a thing – a natural phenomenon – is one factor in undermining resistance to their negative consequences. But, of course, financial markets are social relations, not things. Moreover, the growth in their power (or, strictly speaking, in the power of actors who operate mainly in the financial markets) over the past generation is partly a result of political and ideological struggles.[21] Thus two crucial stages in the emancipation of financial capitalism in Britain were the abolition of exchange controls in 1979 and the deregulation of the City of London (the Big Bang) in 1986, both measures introduced by the Thatcher government as part of its project of restructuring the British economy along neo-liberal lines.

Britain is exceptional among the advanced capitalist countries in the relative economic weight of its financial sector, but on the world stage the United States has played a major role in facilitating the rise of the financial markets. Peter Gowan has argued that the US responded to the collapse of the Bretton Woods system by promoting in its place what he calls the Dollar Wall Street Regime. The role of the dollar, liberated from the old gold-exchange standard in 1971, in underpinning the international monetary system gave the US enormous political and economic leverage, while the new world of floating currencies encouraged international financial speculation in which American investment banks were particularly well-placed to flourish. Meanwhile the axis binding together Wall Street, the

US Treasury, and the international financial institutions promotes the policies of the Washington Consensus, which open up national economies to foreign investment and make them more vulnerable to the fluctuations of the financial markets, and thus more dependent on this axis.[22]

This brings us to what has become one of the chronic features of the neo-liberal era – the 'emerging market' financial crash. Among the most prominent victims of this phenomenon have been Mexico (1994–5), East Asia (1997–8), Russia (1998), and Argentina (2001–). One of the main demands made of states undergoing structural adjustment is that they liberalize their capital account – i.e. allow the free movement of capital across their borders.[23] Countries that are deemed to be a hopeful prospect by the financial markets enjoy a massive inflow of capital. This is in fact a dubious benefit, since (as in the East Asian case, for example) the flood of foreign capital tends to encourage massive over-investment and the development of large-scale over-capacity, depressing profitability. When foreign investors begin to get a whiff of this, the result is panic, and as rapid and large-scale a flight of capital as there had previously been an inflow. The effect is to precipitate the economy affected into deep recession, though the repercussions can be on a much larger scale. According to one estimate, the Asian crisis and its backwash cut $2 trillion off global output in 1998–2000, representing maybe six per cent of world gross domestic product.[24]

Defenders of the Washington Consensus tend to represent these crises as consequences of the cultural and institutional defects of the afflicted societies. The classic case of this is provided by Western denunciations of 'crony capitalism' after the East Asian crisis, as if corrupt links between politicians, bureaucrats, and corporate executives were a Japanese or Korean monopoly. The collapse of Enron in the winter of 2001–2 – one of the flagships of the Wall Street bubble, its stockmarket valuation plummeted from $70 billion to virtually zero in the course of a year, wiping out the savings of its own employees and threatening those of millions of other workers whose pension funds had invested heavily in Enron – exposed a web of fraud extending from the corporation's head offices through the banking, accounting, and insurance industries and deep into Washington. No less than 212 of the 248 members of Congress serving on committees enquiring into the scandal turned out to have taken money from Enron or its disgraced auditors Arthur Andersen.[25] Other major scandals followed at once feted corporations such as WorldCom.

The same Northern-based speculative capitalism responsible for the Enron and WorldCom scams has played a central role in causing the emerging market financial crashes. What Jeffrey Winters writes about capital flight from South-East Asia in 1997 is true of all the crises of the neo-liberal era:

> The chain reaction was set in motion by currency traders and managers of large pools of portfolio capital who operate under intense competitive pressures that cause them to behave in a manner that is objectively irrational and destructive for the whole system, especially the countries involved, but subjectively both rational and necessary for any hope of individual survival.[26]

The 'rescues' mounted by the IMF and the G7 after emerging market crashes typically indemnify financial speculators for the consequences of their gambles and thereby create what conservative bankers tend to denounce as 'moral hazard' by encouraging investors to undertake even more risky ventures in future. More important still, the terms on which new lending is offered to the governments of the affected countries require them to take yet more doses of neo-liberalism. The effect is both to help foreign investors to cherry-pick the most profitable assets, often at bargain-basement prices thanks to the slump, and to make the economy concerned yet more vulnerable to the ups and downs of the financial markets. Thus, as we have already seen, the disease is offered as a cure of the ills it has caused.

This pattern is encouraging growing scepticism about the neo-classical orthodoxy according to which financial markets can do no wrong. This, at any rate is what the Efficient Market Hypothesis asserts. It was summed up by George Gibson as long ago as 1883: 'when shares become publicly known in an open market, the value which they acquire may be regarded as the judgement of the best intelligence concerning them.'[27] This 'hypothesis' offers a splendid refutation of any claim that neo-classical economics is a neutral science. It is reminiscent of Voltaire's Dr Pangloss, who never wearied of declaring, whatever the catastrophe, that all is for the best in this best of possible worlds. Other relatively mainstream economists are unwilling to go to the same extreme of complacency. Thus Stiglitz, in technical work that earned him the 2001 Nobel Prize for Economics, has shown that, once the premisses of general equilibrium theory are slightly varied by dropping the assumption that economic actors are perfectly informed, financial markets are not self-correcting: in particular, asymmetries in information between borrowers and lenders may lead banks to set interest rates at levels that attract speculators and deny credit to good firms. He and Andrew Weiss conclude: 'The usual result of economic theorizing: that prices clear markets, is model specific and is not a general theory of markets – unemployment and credit rationing are not phantasms.'[28]

Looming behind such arguments is the huge shadow of Maynard Keynes. His *General Theory of Employment Interest and Money* (1936) involves a stinging critique of the irrationality of financial markets, including a famous comparison of them with a casino.[29] The other side to this critique is that capitalism is basically a healthy system: provided the state intervenes to regulate financial markets and smooth out the ups and downs of the economic cycle, capitalism is the best system of production.

In the Keynesian era – roughly, between the 1940s and the 1970s – the role of the state took the form primarily of the management of effective demand in order to maintain full employment and of mildly redistributive taxation that, in funding historically high levels of welfare spending, helped to perform this stabilizing function (though, in fact, it was the very high level of *arms* expenditure that was mainly responsible for the long period of economic growth that Western capitalism enjoyed after the Second World War).[30]

National demand management in any case seems less viable in the era of globalization, but one of the main thrusts of the anti-globalization movement has been to come up with other ways of regulating financial markets. James Tobin originally proposed a tax on foreign exchange transactions both 'to throw some sand in the wheels of our excessively efficient financial markets' and to 'restore to national economies and governments some fraction of the short-term autonomy they enjoyed before currency convertibility became so easy'.[31] For movements like ATTAC, the Tobin Tax has the advantage of not merely slowing down global finance, but also generating resources that could be used to fund Third World development: on one estimate, a tax on every foreign exchange transaction of 0.25 per cent would have produced a revenue of nearly $300 billion in 1995.[32]

Considered on its own, then, the tax is a method of reforming capitalism – and in particular of rehabilitating national capitalisms. It implies what one might call a relatively superficial critique of capitalism, one that locates the problem in what Tobin calls 'unanchored' financial markets, rather than at the level of the system itself.[33] Even as enthusiastic a supporter as Heikki Patomäki acknowledges that the Tobin Tax does not address 'the problem of financial *short-termism* as a whole' or 'the *governance of credit and investments* in the global political economy'.[34] The latter issue in particular poses the question of the nature of the system itself, and for that we need, not Keynes or Tobin, but Marx.

The perpetual motion machine

Marx claims that capitalism has two fundamental features – the *exploitation of wage-labour* and the *competitive accumulation of capital*. These in turn correspond to the two relationships constitutive of capitalism – respectively, that between capital and labour and that among capitals themselves. Both are conflictual: the 'vertical' relationship between capital and labour arises from the antagonism that necessarily obtains between exploiter and exploited, while the 'horizontal' relationship among capitals consists in the competitive struggle among the exploiters over the distribution of profits they have jointly extracted from the working class. 'Capital' in the singular, which refers both to the totality of relationships that constitute the capitalist mode of production and to the capitalist class as a collectivity, is therefore to be distinguished from the plurality of 'capitals', the individual units of the system that struggle to exploit and to accumulate.[35]

Treating capitalism as a social system founded on exploitation serves a number of functions. Here are five of them:

1   Marx insists that *class antagonism* is not a secondary or accidental feature of capitalism but defines its very nature: capital is at fundamental odds with the wage-labourers it employs, who comprise all those compelled by their economic circumstances to sell their labour-power and to work under supervision, irrespective of whether they do so in industry or services, or as blue- or white-collar workers.

2   To say, as Marx does in his theory of surplus-value, that the profits sought by capital derive from the

labour of the workers they employ, is to assert that capitalism rests on a profound *injustice*: those who do the actual work of producing goods and services are compelled to labour also to support capitalists whose claim on the fruits of production derives solely from their control of productive resources.[36]

3   Marx's theory of surplus-value *historically situates* capitalism with respect to earlier class-based modes of production: whereas, in these social systems, exploitation depended on a class of unfree producers (whether slaves or some sort of dependent peasantry), under capitalism workers are free in the sense that they are not legally required to serve their exploiters – instead, it is their lack of economic independence that compels them to work for the capitalists on unequal terms that lead to their exploitation.

4   This exploitive set-up implies that it is the workers who are the source of *creativity* under capitalism: capitalists' creativity is at best of a second-order sort, consisting in the ability to take advantage of others' innovations and to get the better of both their work-force and their rivals (this is the rational kernel of theories of entrepreneurship).[37]

5   The theory of capitalist exploitation indicates the *limits* of the system, in the sense that capitalists as a class can only increase their total profits by reducing the real wages or increasing the productivity of the working class: this relation of dependence means that workers are not just exploited – they are powerful as well.

But Marx's theory of capitalism is incomplete so long as it is confined to the vertical relationship between capital and labour. The horizontal relationship between capitals is important for two reasons. First, Marx argues that the competitive struggle of capitals explains *why* exploitation and accumulation are chronic features of capitalism as an economic system. Capitalism is sufficiently competitive for each individual capital to be under constant pressure to reduce its costs of production in order to maintain or even to increase its market share. A benevolent capitalist who paid his workers wages that broadly corresponded to the amount of value that they created would soon find himself out of business. For, directly or indirectly, from profits are funded the investments through which individual capitals expand and/or improve their productive capacity. It is this process of increasing productivity and capacity by the reinvestment of profits that Marx (following Adam Smith) called the accumulation of capital. This is a competitive process because the drive to accumulate is externally induced: the pressure of their rivals compels capitals to improve their methods of production. Marx offers a *structural* theory of capital accumulation: the impulse to accumulate is not to be explained by individual psychology or by the cultural processes explored by Max Weber in *The Protestant Ethic and the Spirit of Capitalism*, but by the structure of compulsions and incentives to which individual capitalists find themselves subjected in the market (though – in principle at any rate – the kind of cultural explanations offered by Weber might help to account for the differential success of particular groups in responding to market disciplines).

Second, seeing capitalism as a system of competitive accumulation helps to explain its *trajectory*. Capitalism is characterized at once by dynamism and by instability. Both these characteristics derive from the competitive struggle among capitals. Productivity-enhancing investments expand the productive powers of humankind. This is the development of the productive forces for which Marx praises capitalism in the *Communist Manifesto* and the *Grundrisse*, even while he distinguishes capitalist relations of production – the historically specific forms of control over productive resources that constitute this mode of production – from the growth in productivity and output of which these relations provide the social framework. But the nature of these production relations also means that the development of the productive forces makes capitalism constitutively liable to crisis.[38] We have already encountered the fundamental mechanism responsible at work in the financial markets, where doing what is individually rational often produces collectively suboptimal outcomes.

Individual capitals invest in improved methods of production in the expectation of obtaining a higher return. The innovator can generally hope to succeed (in the short term at least) because, by lowering his costs of production below average costs in the sector, he can either undercut his rivals by cutting the price of his products and selling more of them or, if he leaves prices unchanged, obtain a higher profit per unit sold. Either way the innovating capital is in a position to put others in the sector under increasing pressure. So they seek to match his innovation. Insofar as they succeed in doing so, average costs of production in the sector will fall. Since the innovator's advantage derived from the difference between his individual costs and the sectoral average, and this difference has now disappeared, so too will his extra profit (what Marx calls 'super-profit', and more recent economists 'technological rent'). Improved productivity generally depends on increasing the plant and equipment that each worker must operate: so the innovation will have been won at the price of a higher investment in plant and equipment per worker (or, as Marx rather unhelpfully puts it, the organic composition of capital rises). But labour is the source of profits. So – unless the rate of exploitation (profits per worker) rises – a larger amount of capital is required to extract the same amount of profit from the workforce. In other words, the rate of profit – the ratio between profits and total investment – falls. The profit-seeking behaviour of individual capitals has thus, once the innovations applied through this behaviour have been generalized, produced a decline in the overall rate of profit.

Extended to the economy as a whole, this mechanism is responsible for what Marx calls the tendency of the general rate of profit to fall. This is only a tendency because it depends on certain conditions obtaining, most (though not all) of which Marx lists – that productivity is raised by saving labour rather than capital, that the rate of exploitation does not increase sufficiently to counteract the effects of the rise in the organic composition of capital (the ratio between investment in means of production and investment in labour-power), or that the means of production do not themselves become cheaper thanks to the productivity-enhancing innovation, once again preventing a fall in the rate of profit (since then the *value* of investment in plant and equipment might have fallen per worker, even if the physical *amount* she operates had risen). But Marx seems to have thought that the most important 'counter-acting effects' are provided by economic crises. A sufficiently pronounced fall in the rate of profit causes capitalists to stop investing and thereby precipitates the economy into a recession. The principal feature of a recession is that capitals either go bankrupt or cut output and employment. The resulting rise in the rate of unemployment reduces workers' bargaining power, placing those who still have jobs under pressure to accept lower wages, longer hours, and worse conditions. This has the effect of increasing the rate of exploitation. At the same time, the stronger capitals can buy up the stocks of bankrupt firms cheap and also absorb the weaker survivors on favourable terms. The value of existing investments is thereby reduced. Together these two processes – a rise in the rate of exploitation and the destruction of capital – increase the mass of profits relative to that of capital. In other words, the rate of profit rises. When profitability has risen sufficiently to stimulate a recovery in investment, economic growth will resume, until the next pronounced fall in the general rate of profit causes another downward turn in this infernal cycle.

Marx's theory of the tendency of the rate of profit to fall is of particular interest because, as it happens, the major capitalist economies began to experience a serious crisis of profitability in the late 1960s. This crisis, however caused, underlies the transition the world economy underwent to an era of slow growth punctuated by global recessions that continues to the present.[39] Marx's own account of the mechanisms responsible for such crises of profitability has proved enormously controversial: it is fair to say that it has been rejected by most conventionally trained economists, even though their reasons for doing so often seem to have more to do with their incomprehension of the distinctive kind of theoretical approach to the capitalist economy that he took than with specific defects of an argument that raises many complex issues.[40] This is not the place to explore these issues, even were I competent to do so. More relevant is the general image that Marx offers of capitalism as a system in which the process of competitive accumulation encourages individual capitals to undertake actions that, while they may in the short term raise their profit-rate, have the longer-term effect of undermining the viability of the system as a whole. Individual profit-seeking produces globally disastrous results. In the rest of this section and in the following one, I explore two contemporary aspects of this paradox, one narrowly economic, the other much broader.

In the first place, one of the driving forces towards crisis in the contemporary world economy is a pronounced tendency towards over-investment. This was, for example, a major feature of the East Asian crisis in the late 1990s. Competition for export markets – intensified by the devaluations of the Chinese renminbi and the Japanese yen in mid-decade – encouraged firms to expand their capacity much more quickly than their profits could grow to match them. The result was massive over-investment and over-capacity. On the eve of the chain of financial crashes that swept through East and South-East Asia in 1997, the *Financial Times* reported:

> At an annual average growth rate of over 20 per cent this decade, investment has been rising about three times as fast

as growth in domestic gross national product, suggesting Asia has been suffering from a serious case of over-investment. Now . . . capacity use is running at very low levels in countries such as China (below 60 per cent), South Korea (below 70 per cent) and Taiwan (72 per cent).[41]

The inflows of speculative capital fuelled this process of expansion, and then, as the consequences of over-investment became clear, by their withdrawal helped to precipitate Asia into deep recession. Precisely the same interaction of speculative financial markets and competition among industrial firms can be seen at work in the rise and fall of the American 'New Economy' during the great US boom of 1992–2000.[42] This boom was made possible by a recovery in profitability from the low-point reached in the early 1980s, a recovery in turn caused by large-scale economic restructuring that eliminated inefficient capitals, a historically unprecedented repression of real wages, and the devaluation of the dollar relative to other major currencies as a result of the 1985 Plaza Accords. But, by the late 1990s, these effects had worked themselves out. In the middle of the decade the Clinton administration switched to a strong dollar policy (designed in part to help the Japanese economy escape from the stagnation that has dogged it since the early 1990s). The rate of return in manufacturing industry began to fall in late 1997, and the sustained drop in unemployment allowed a moderate rise in real wages. What kept the boom going for three more years was the response of the Federal Reserve Board to the panic that swept world financial markets after the Russian collapse in August 1998 seemed to portend a chain-reaction of crashes in 'emergent markets' that would spread to the centres of global capitalism. The Fed under Alan Greenspan slashed interest rates and took other steps (for example, organizing the rescue of the hedge fund Long-Term Capital Management) designed to bolster confidence.

This policy of what Robert Brenner calls 'stock market Keynesianism' (evidence that the nation-state still plays a major role in the era of globalization) succeeded all too well.[43] American financial markets continued to soar into the stratosphere till March 2000, fuelled in part by inflows of capital seeking the security of the United States. The rise in the value of their stockmarket investments encouraged American firms and affluent households to run down their savings and borrow massively, generating gigantic financial imbalances – in particular, unprecedented levels of private sector indebtedness and a record balance of payments deficit.[44] The same climate encouraged firms to expand their investments in the expectation that their profits would continue to grow sufficiently to justify these decisions. These expectations proved to be mistaken: post-tax profits fell as a share of US national income from more than 12 per cent in 1997 to 8 per cent three years later.[45]

As a result, key sectors of the American and indeed the world economy were confronted with growing problems of over-investment and over-capacity. The industries worst affected were in many cases those most closely identified with the 'New Economy', notably technology, media, and telecommunications. It was this reality that underlay the collapse in this sector's share prices in spring 2000. Nearly two years later the *Financial Times* reported:

> According to the European Information Technology Observatory, investment in telecommunications rose between 1997 and 2000 by about 20 per cent in the US and about 50 per cent in Western Europe.
>
> A large proportion of that investment does appear to have been wasted. One estimate suggests that in the telecommunications industry alone, over the past four years, about \$1,000 bn (£690 bn) was, in effect, thrown away, for example in laying fibre-optic cables that may never be used.

In information technology generally, the legacy of past over-investment is everywhere. Scott McNealy, the chief executive of Sun Microsystems, has said he is having to compete against his own products, sold off as bankrupt stock, at as little as 10 per cent of list price.[46]

As in the case of the Japanese 'bubble economy' of the late 1980s, this overhang of bad investments left over from the boom may make it difficult for the Fed's policy of dramatic interest-rate cuts to stimulate the resumption of rapid growth. But more interesting here than any immediate prognosis of the development of the world economy, is the dynamic revealed by the evolution of the American boom of the 1990s. The same logic was at work there that was also present in the Asian crisis: financial speculation – underwritten by the state – encouraged rival capitals to expand their productive capacity far more rapidly than the growth in profits required to justify these investments. It is this process of uncontrolled accumulation, driven by competition and speculation, that is responsible for the collapse of two of the three largest zones of advanced capitalism into recession over the past decade. From this point of view, the role of financial markets is less as an autonomous source of instability, more as one dimension of a set of interconnected processes driving capitalist economies towards crisis. Marx's own analysis of what he called the 'credit system' seems apposite here: the development of credit money and its availability through the banks and financial markets make it possible to sustain the accumulation process for longer than would be otherwise feasible, but the effect is to postpone – and often to intensify – the onset of the underlying economic contradictions.[47] The financial markets, backed by the Fed, helped to sustain the American boom but that boom was not merely a speculative artefact: it depended on a real, if limited recovery in profitability, and, when the rate of profit began to fall, the collapse of the boom was only a matter of time.

Accumulation and catastrophe

But the same logic of competitive accumulation is at work in other arenas. By far and away the most important of these concerns the natural environment on which all life on the planet depends. In his outstanding environmental history of the twentieth century John McNeill distinguishes between two evolutionary strategies – adaptability to changing circumstances, pursued, for example, by some species of rat, and 'supreme adaptation to existing circumstances', represented by sharks, who rely on the plentiful supply of other sea creatures that they can hunt and eat. McNeill continues:

> In the twentieth century, societies often pursued the shark strategy amid a global ecology ever more unstable, and hence ever more suited for rats. We energetically pursued adaptations to evanescent circumstances. Perhaps a quarter of us live in ways fully predicated on stable climate, cheap energy and water, and rapid population and economic growth. Most of the rest of us understandably aspire to live in such ways. Our institutions and ideologies too are by now built on the same premises.
>
> Those premises are not too flimsy, but they are temporary. Climate has changed little for 10,000 years, since the retreat of the last ice age; it is changing fast now. Cheap energy is a feature of the fossil fuel age, roughly since 1820. Cheap water, for those who enjoy it, dates to the nineteenth century except in a few favoured settings. Rapid population growth dates from the middle of the eighteenth century, and fast economic growth from about 1870. To regard these circumstances as enduring and normal, and to depend on their continuation, is an interesting gamble.[48]

These circumstances are mutually dependent: population growth can only be sustained if agricultural production – contrary to Malthus's predictions – grows sufficiently to feed the extra mouths, as it has so far managed to do.[49] They are, however, not necessarily mutually compatible: to take the most obvious case, the rising temperature of the earth as a result of a build-up in green-house gases caused by human actions – for example, fossil fuel burning and deforestation leading to rising levels of carbon dioxide in the atmosphere – is likely to have drastic consequences for the life of humans and other species in the twenty-first century. In exploring the causes of these changes, McNeill distinguishes between 'clusters' – 'com-binations of simultaneous technical, organizational, and social innovations':

> Early industrial clusters were built around water-powered textile mills and then factories and steam engines. After the mid-twentieth century the dominant cluster emerged as coal, iron, steel, and railroads: heavy-engineering indus-tries centred in smokestack cities. Call it the 'coketown cluster' in honour of Charles Dickens's Coketown . . . The next cluster coalesced in the 1920s and 1930s and pre-dominated from the 1940s (helped along by World War II) until the 1990s: assembly lines, oil, electricity, automobiles and aircraft, chemicals, plastics, and fertilizers – all organ-ized by big corporations. I will dub that the 'motown cluster' in honour of Detroit, the world centre of motor vehicle manufacture. The coketown cluster and the motown cluster each spurred the emergence of giant cor-porations in North America, Europe, and Japan and the relative efficiency and returns to scale enjoyed by these corporations in turn helped to advance each cluster; tech-nological systems and business structures coevolved.[50]

McNeill speculates that a new cluster may have emerged in the 1990s, possibly centred on genetic engineering and information technology.[51] However that may be, it seems undeniable that this narrative of socio-technical clusters is another way of telling the story of capitalism in its suc-cessive transformations from the Industrial Revolution to the contemporary era of neo-liberal globalization. McNeill himself prefers to give a greater explanatory role to ideas, arguing that, for example, the environmental catastrophes that afflicted the Soviet Union had ideological roots: 'Deep in Marxism is the belief that nature exists to be harnessed by labour.'[52] The much more nuanced attitude towards nature displayed by the founders of Marxism is suggested by the following remarks by Engels. After arguing that man through his labour '*masters*' his environment, Engels goes on to write:

> Let us not, however, flatter ourselves overmuch on account of our human victories over nature. For each such victory nature takes its revenge on us. Each victory, it is true, in the first place brings about the results we expected, but in the second and third places it has quite different, unforeseen effects which only too often cancel the first. The people who, in Mesopotamia, Greece, Asia Minor and elsewhere, destroyed the forests to obtain cultivable land, never dreamed that by removing along with the forests the collecting centres and reservoirs of moisture they were laying the basis for the present forlorn state of those countries. When the Italians of the Alps used up the pine forests on the southern slopes, so carefully cherished on the northern slopes, they had no inkling that by doing so they were cutting at the roots of the dairy industry in their region; they had still less inkling that they were thereby depriving their mountain springs of water for the greater part of the year, and making it possible for them to pour still more furious torrents on the plains during the rainy seasons. Those who spread the potato in Europe were not aware that with these farinaceous tubers they were at the same time spreading scrofula. Thus at each step we are reminded that we by no means rule over nature like a conqueror over a foreign people, like someone standing outside nature – but that we, with flesh, blood and brain, belong to nature, and exist in its midst, and that all our mastery of it consists in the fact that we have the advantage over all other creatures of being able to learn its laws and apply it correctly.[53]

Engels here identifies precisely the dialectic of unintended consequences at work in the processes of environmental destruction – global warming, for example – that are now becoming evident. Marx's own attitude to the natural world was similarly complex: alongside the notion of human mastery of nature can be found other themes – for example, an enduring preoccupation with humankind's place in the physical world and a growing concern about the environmental damage caused by capitalist agricultural methods.[54] What encouraged the rulers of the USSR to select from this diverse and perhaps ambiguous heritage those aspects of classical Marxism that seemed to support the idea that nature is something to be conquered and controlled? The answer has more to do with power and interests than with ideology conceived as an autonomous force. The more the Stalinist system recedes into the past, the more it becomes clear that it reproduced – in an extreme form induced by the intensity of internal conflicts and the pressure of geopolitical competition – the tendencies to treat nature as an inexhaustible source of raw material and energy sources that both the coketown and motown clusters presupposed.[55]

The present situation is in any case one where the major forms of environmental destruction arise from the logic of capital accumulation. On the one hand, the motown cluster is very far from being a thing of the past. Quite to the contrary, the giant fossil fuel corporations – the companies that dominate the world's oil, gas, coal, car, road construction, and rubber industries – represent an enormously powerful constellation of economic interests. Having bitterly opposed the feeble targets for reducing greenhouse emissions agreed in the 1997 Kyoto protocol, the American fossil fuel corporations successfully backed a presidential candidate, George W. Bush, one of whose first major acts after entering the White House was to denounce the protocol. Congressional investigations into the Enron scandal exposed how the company had manipulated the deregulated Californian energy industry by, for example, shutting down plants, and exporting power, thereby creating artificial shortages that boosted prices and profits. Enron and other energy traders also engaged in scams like 'roundtripping' – phoney sales that increased turnover and pushed up prices. The Bush administration used the resulting energy crisis in California to demand reduced environmental controls on oil-drilling in the Pacific Northwest. On the other hand, a handful of multinational corporations led by the five 'Gene Giants' – AstraZeneca, DuPont, Monsanto, Novartis, and Aventis – are using the latest technologies to drive through the large-scale introduction of genetically modified organisms, with unpredictable and possibly disastrous consequences, including the spread of food allergies, an increase in the already serious problem of species resistant to antibiotics, and the development of new viruses. The biotechnology corporations' positively obscene aspiration to control the entire food chain is indicated by the development of 'Terminator' technologies, thanks to which genetically modified seeds would produce infertile plants, thus rendering farmers permanently dependent on the suppliers of these seeds.[56]

To see capitalism as the source of contemporary threats to the environment is not, by any means, to treat nature as merely a social construct, the effect of human manipulation. In his masterpiece *Late Victorian Holocausts* Mike Davis sensitively reconstructs the interaction of the El Niño–Southern Oscillation (ENSO) – the recurrent oscillations in oceanic temperatures across the Pacific and the patterns of wet and dry weather they cause – with the increasingly integrated liberal world economy of the late nineteenth century. He shows how, in combination with the erosion of traditional mechanisms for coping with famine under the influence of the Western colonial powers and the increasing subordination of peasant agriculture to the rhythms of the world market, El Niño droughts led to appalling human catastrophes in Asia and Latin America: in India alone between 12 and 30 million people died in the droughts of 1876–9 and 1896–1902. At the same time '[t]he great Victorian famines were forcing houses and accelerators of the very socio-economic forces that ensured their occurrence in the first place': the famine-induced mass pauperization of the great Asiatic civilizations helped to generate the global inequalities in income and wealth between First and Third Worlds that are now taken for granted but were scarcely visible two centuries ago. 'From the standpoint of political ecology,' Davis writes, 'the vulnerability of tropical agriculturalists to extreme climate events was magnified by simultaneous restructurings of household and village linkages to regional production systems, world commodity markets and the colonial (or dependent) state.' ENSO is a set of autonomous natural processes whose existence long predates and will presumably also survive the existence of capitalism: it was only in a particular social and historical context, provided by the integration of peasant societies in the capitalist world market, the disruptive impact of the imperial powers, and the hegemony of liberal ideology, that these processes had such ghastly consequences.[57]

Human intervention in the physical world is inherently liable to the dialectic of unintended consequences portrayed by Engels.[58] He imagined that humans would, with the help of the natural sciences, be able to remedy these consequences when they proved to be damaging. But this process is greatly inhibited by the current domination of capitalist relations of production, which encourage the employment of scientific knowledge to render the physical world (including such abstract properties as genes) as comprehensively fungible and usable. The logic of competitive accumulation thus not merely causes profound economic crises; it is the main force behind the increasingly threatening process of environmental destruction. Trapped in the competitive struggle to gain an edge over their rivals, capitals are driving collectively towards an outcome that portends planetary disaster. Susan George has powerfully evoked this logic:

It is also chimerical to think that the transnationals and the rich countries will change their behaviour in the least when they finally understand that they will destroy the life of the planet on which we must all live. In my view they couldn't stop even if they wanted to, even for the future of their own children. Capitalism is like the famous bicycle that must always go forwards or fall over and firms are competing to see who can pedal faster before smashing against the wall.[59]

The sword of Leviathan

The argument so far has proceeded as if capitalism could be conceived simply as an economic system, even if its consequences, as we have just seen, extend much more broadly. Since 9–11, however, it has become quite clear that such a perspective is wholly inadequate, that the present system embraces geopolitics as well as economics, and that the competitive processes that threaten such destructive consequences involve not merely the economic struggle for markets, but military and diplomatic rivalries among states. The view, put forward by Third Way ideologues such as Anthony Giddens and Ulrich Beck, that globalization was transforming the liberal democratic state into 'the state without enemies' now seems simply ludicrous in the light of George W. Bush's proclamation of a global state of war on 20 September 2001: 'Americans should not expect one battle, but a lengthy campaign, unlike any other that we have ever seen . . . Every nation, in every region, now has a decision to make. Either you are with us, or you are with the terrorists.'[60]

One of globalization's more vulgar boosters, the *New York Times* columnist Thomas Friedman, proved much more realistic than Beck and Giddens when he declared in a much-quoted passage:

The hidden hand of the market will never work without a hidden fist.

Markets function and flourish only when property rights are secured and can be enforced, which, in turn, requires a political framework protected and backed by military power . . . Indeed, McDonald's cannot flourish without McDonnell Douglas, the designer of the US Air Force F-15. And the hidden fist that keeps the world safe for Silicon Valley's technologies to flourish is called the US Army, Air Force, Navy and Marine Corps.[61]

This fist has hardly been kept hidden lately. The rapid assertion of US military power to topple the Taliban regime in Afghanistan in October–November 2001 left the world shaken by this demonstration of American ascendancy (though subsequent fighting suggested that the Taliban and its al-Qaeda allies had not been destroyed but had withdrawn from the cities to wage a guerrilla war in the mountains of Afghanistan and Pakistan). The *Financial Times* calculated that the $379 billion planned US defence spending in 2003 'exceeds the total combined military budgets of the next 14 biggest spenders – including Japan, Western Europe, Russia and China'.[62] The historian Paul Kennedy wrote a bestseller in the late 1980s predicting that 'the United States now runs the risk, so familiar to historians of the rise and fall of Great Powers, of what might roughly be called "imperial overstretch"', as US strategic commitments outran its economic capacities.[63] After the fall of Kabul Kennedy could hardly contain his awe for American military supremacy. After an almost loving description of the Pentagon's most important single instrument of power projection – the twelve carrier battle groups, each with 'the capacity to deal out death and destruction across most of our globe', he declared: 'The larger lesson [of the Afghan war] – and one stupefying to the Russian and Chinese military, worrying to the Indians, and disturbing to proponents of a common European defence policy – is that in military terms there is only one player in the field who counts.'[64]

But in whose interests is this immense power exercised? The passage cited from Friedman has almost a vulgar

Marxist ring about it; moreover, it implies that American military might serves to maintain capitalist property relations irrespective of where they are located, or of the nationality of the capitalists who benefit from them. Such at any rate is the view expressed by Michael Hardt and Toni Negri in one of the influential texts of the anti-capitalist movement, *Empire*. For Hardt and Negri, imperialism has been supplanted by Empire, a novel form of capitalist domination that 'establishes no territorial centre of power and does not rely on fixed boundaries and barriers . . . In this smooth space of Empire, there is no *place* of power – it is everywhere and nowhere.'[65] Consequently, according to Negri,

> it is no longer possible to talk about 'American imperialism'. Quite simply there exist groups, elites that control the keys of exploitation and thus the keys to the war machine, and who attempt to impose themselves at the world level. Naturally, this process is highly contradictory and will necessarily be so for a long time to come. For the moment, it is above all the North American bosses who exercise this domination. Immediately behind them, there are the Europeans, the Russians, the Chinese: they are there to support them, or to undermine them, or even to be ready to take over a change of leadership – but this change remains superficial since at the basis what is still and always at work is capital, collective capital.[66]

Though formulated in Marxist language, Hardt's and Negri's analysis bears a striking resemblance to more mainstream theories of political globalization. According to such theories, the post-Cold War era has seen the emergence of forms of 'global governance' that transcend national interests, even those of the strongest state.[67] Contemporary perceptions of US power indeed seem to oscillate between the frustration and fear expressed at evidence of American 'unilateralism', especially since the younger Bush entered the White House, and the belief that this power is progressively becoming the agent of an impersonal structure, whether that structure be conceptualized as the emerging forms of 'cosmopolitan democracy' or as the global domination of 'collective capital'.

The great difficulty for the theorists of global governance is that the world distribution of political and military power both is highly unequal and closely corresponds to the also grossly unequal distribution of economic power. Indeed, neo-liberal ideologues are increasingly willing openly to acknowledge the necessity of a unilateral assertion of Western power vis-à-vis the rest of the world, in other words, of imperialism. One of the clearest statements of this view has come from Robert Cooper, a Foreign Office official close to Tony Blair:

> All the conditions for imperialism are there, but both the supply and demand for imperialism have dried up. And yet the weak still need the strong and the strong still need an orderly world. A world in which the efficient and well governed export stability and liberty, and which is open to investment and growth – all of this seems eminently desirable.
>
> What is needed then is a new kind of imperialism, one acceptable to a world of human rights and cosmopolitan values. We can already discern its outline: an imperialism which brings order and organization, but which rests today on the voluntary principle.[68]

Imperial rulers and their apologists have always claimed to give their subjects 'order and organization'. *'Solitudinem faciunt, pacem appellant'* – They create a wilderness and call it peace: the great Roman historian Tacitus put this riposte by the victims of empire into the mouth of the first-century Caledonian leader Calgacus.[69] An astonishing contemporary philippic against the American empire was recently launched by Chalmers Johnson, a leading American scholar of modern Asia in his book *Blowback*. Johnson – hitherto a figure firmly in the academic and political mainstream – develops a withering critique of American foreign policy. He dismisses 'globalization' as 'an esoteric term for what in the nineteenth century was simply called imperialism', and places the East Asian crisis firmly at Washington's door: 'The economic crisis at the end of the century had its origins in an American project to open up and make over the economies of its satellites and dependencies in East Asia. Its purpose was to diminish them as competitors and to assert the primacy of the United States as the global hegemonic power.'[70]

Developing a comprehensive analysis of 'blowback' – 'the unintended consequences of policies that were kept secret from the American people', Johnson comes close to predicting 11 September:

> Terrorism by definition strikes at the innocent in order to draw attention to the sins of the invulnerable. The innocent of the twenty-first century are going to harvest unexpected blowback disasters from the imperialist escapades of recent decades. Although most Americans may be largely ignorant of what was, and still is, being done in their name, all are likely to pay a steep price – individually and collectively – for their nation's continued efforts to dominate the global scene.[71]

Johnson's analysis of the roots of the American empire is the opposite of Friedman's. Whereas the latter comes close to Hardt's and Negri's view of US military power as a tool of global capital, Johnson reduces the economic to the political: 'Marx and Lenin were mistaken about the nature of imperialism. It is not the contradictions of capitalism that lead to imperialism but imperialism that breeds some of the most important contradictions of capitalism. When these contradictions ripen, as they must, they create devastating economic crises.'[72] But both these extreme positions are mistaken. The Marxist theory of imperialism is capable of offering a non-reductive account of how the logic of competitive accumulation analysed in the earlier parts of this chapter can be extended to cover geopolitical conflicts and military power.[73] This theory was formulated at the beginning of the twentieth century in order to render intelligible a world economy unified by industrial capitalism.[74] It involves three central propositions:

1 This unification was achieved on a highly unequal basis (what Trotsky called 'uneven and combined development'), involving the economic and military domination of the globe by a handful of Western capitalist powers.

2 The development of industrial capitalism within these states induced a process of structural transformation: on the one hand, economic power became increasingly concentrated with the emergence of large corporations and the tendency of money and productive capital to fuse into what Rudolf Hilferding called 'finance capital'; on the other hand, these large firms tended to combine with their nation states into, as Nikolai Bukharin put it, 'state capitalist trusts'.

3 The forms of competition consequently changed: economic rivalries became inseparable from military and territorial conflicts: the resulting economico-political struggles among the leading imperialist powers were the driving force behind the two world wars.

How well do these three assertions hold up a century after their first formulation? None can be accepted without any modification, but they retain a substantial measure of truth. Let us consider them in order.

1 We still live in a world of crushing global inequalities. The colonial empires long ago disappeared, but the consequence of their downfall has not been the disappearance of the vast economic gulf between what we now call North and South.[75] Formal colonialism was a feature of a world divided among a plurality of rival national–imperial blocs based primarily in the Eurasian continent. The final implosion of old Europe during the Second World War led to the emergence of a

new geopolitical division, between two superpower blocs, the global empire of the United States and the more restricted Eurasian domain of the Soviet Union. The European empires proved unsustainable in this new environment, but the liberated colonies mostly found themselves still outsiders in a world dominated by the Western capitalist bloc and the USSR. The flows of foreign direct investment since 1945 have been concentrated very largely in the OECD bloc itself, with a handful of the most advanced 'emerging market' economies fitfully included in this golden circle since the 1970s. Much of the world – for example, the bulk of sub-Saharan Africa – is subject to what Michael Mann has called 'ostracizing imperialism', deemed not even worth exploiting:

> most of the world's poorest countries are not being significantly integrated into transnational capitalism, but are 'ostracized' by a capitalism which regards them as too risky for investment and trade. It is conventional to describe this economic divide as being between 'North' and 'South', though this is too crude a division and is not strictly geographical. Much of Russia, China and the ex-Soviet Central Asian republics are classified as 'South', while Australia and New Zealand are 'North'.[76]

On the other hand, in the course of the twentieth century the accumulation process did spread, albeit highly unevenly, to the Third World. The dependency theorists of the 1960s and 1970s (for example, Andre Gunder Frank, Samir Amin, and Immanuel Wallerstein) were wrong when they argued that capitalist global domination meant only 'the development of underdevelopment' in the periphery. Varying combinations of state intervention and foreign direct investment allowed some states to become significant exporters of manufactured goods in the post-war era. But only very rarely did this process lead to entire societies joining the First World: among the chief examples of this happening are Spain, Greece, Portugal, southern Ireland,

and South Korea, all predominantly peasant societies till
they began to undergo rapid industrialization in the 1960s.
Much more frequently, pockets of capitalist development
often highly integrated in the world economy coexist with
vast pools of misery in city and countryside alike: this is
the pattern in Latin America, South Asia, and China.[77]
And, as South Korea discovered in the late 1990s, even the
most developed 'emerging market' economies are still
subject to decision-making processes dominated by the US
and the other leading capitalist states: indeed, the neo-
liberal programmes of structural adjustment pushed
through by the IMF and the World Bank in the 1980s and
1990s specifically targeted those features of the 'emerging
market' economies (for example, the relatively high levels
of state intervention) that had made their industrialization
possible in the first place.

2 The structure of capitalist power in the advanced
economies also experienced both change and continuity.
The nationally organized capitalisms that prevailed during
the first half of the twentieth century have undoubtedly
been cracked open as the world economy has experienced
a significant process of integration. But this process is a
highly uneven one: economic globalization has gone
much further through the integration of financial markets
than it has at the level of trade or investment. Multinational
corporations, largely still based in the OECD countries,
have emerged as the most powerful economic actors, but
the more extreme claims that global capitalism has broken
free of the nation-state are largely false. To take what
appears to be the most important counter-example, the
limited transfer of sovereignty to the European Union has
been a vehicle of distinct and sometimes at least partially
contradictory national projects, notably those of France
and Germany, and has been intended to give the European
powers collective leverage against the United States: this has
been most successful in the area of trade, where the lobby-
ing efforts of business interests demonstrate a lively sense
of the enduring economic importance of the state.[78]

3 The single most important change in the structure of imperialism in the second half of the twentieth century was the partial dissociation of economic and military competition. Before 1945, economic and geopolitical conflict tended to be mutually reinforcing. At the beginning of the century, Britain was confronted with two challengers to both its industrial and its naval supremacy, the United States and Germany. It ended up reluctantly allying with one to defeat the other, and lost its leading role anyway. Economic and political concerns also fused in the case of the two challengers: in both world wars German imperialism sought to employ its military might to carve out a zone in Central and Eastern Europe in which it would gain privileged access to markets, resources, and labour; the US used the second war to ensure that the outcome would be an open world economy in which American capital and goods could freely flow. After 1945 the patterns of competition diverged: the Soviet Union was a geopolitical and ideological rival to the US, but not, on the whole, an economic threat. The Cold War gave Washington both the incentive and the means to unite the other major capitalist states – Western Europe and Japan – under its political and military leadership. The long post-war boom saw Germany and Japan emerge as serious economic competitors to the US, but this conflict remained relatively muted politically, in large part because of Bonn's and Tokyo's dependence on the American military shield.

The collapse of the Soviet bloc in 1989–91 brought another kaleidoscopic shift to this pattern, though one in which certain relationships persisted. Of course, what one might call superpower imperialism – the partition of the world between two geopolitical and ideological blocs – vanished. But the partial dissociation of economic and political competition remained: America's main geopolitical rivals – most obviously Russia and China – were not significant economic competitors (yet); at the same time, the chronic US balance of payments deficit helped to ensure that conflict over international trade among the 'Quad' of leading economic powers (the US, EU, Japan, and Canada) remained constant and intermittently intense. Three features of this situation are worth noting. First, as we have already seen, the US military lead over other powers grew enormously, partly because of the implosion of the other (though always much weaker) superpower, and partly as a spin-off from the sheer size and technological sophistication of the American economy. Second, successive US administrations made intense efforts to ensure both that America remained top of both the economic and geopolitical series and that no other major capitalist state developed into a political challenger: a case in point was the way in which the Clinton administration used the Balkan Wars of the 1990s to maintain the US role as the leading politico-military power on the European continent, intervening to impose a settlement in Bosnia and to expand NATO into Central and Eastern Europe.[79] Third, a projection of current trends suggests that the two series may soon meet in China. Rapid economic growth could transform what is already a regional power into a strategic challenger. Hence the ambivalence towards China of American elites, for whom the country's economic dynamism since its reintegration into the world market simultaneously confirms the superiority of market capitalism over other social systems and poses a longer-term threat.

The resulting geopolitical set-up has been well characterized by Samuel Huntington as 'a strange hybrid, a uni-multipolar system with one superpower and several major powers. The settlement of key international issues requires action by the single superpower but always with some combination of other major states; the single superpower can, however, veto action on key issues by combinations of other states.'[80] This state of affairs helps to explain some of the peculiarities of contemporary geopolitics. As theorists of global governance have rightly argued, the post-Cold War era has been marked by an unprecedentedly high level of policy coordination among the leading capitalist states, expressed in a fountain of multilateralist acronyms – UN, IMF, WTO, NATO, EU, G8, G7 – and an ideological shift away from the primacy of national sovereignty, implied, for example, by the assertion of the Western powers of a right to 'humanitarian intervention' where they see fit. This institutionalized process of policy coordination performs a triple function: it allows the US to brigade together the other major Western powers behind its initiatives; provides an arena in which disputes among the leading capitalist states can be expressed and compromises reached; and offers a means by which they can collectively impose their will on the large majority of states effectively excluded from their counsels. All in all, this amounts not to the transcendence of inter-state conflict, but its pursuit on another terrain.

The hybrid nature of the present geopolitical structure helps also to explain the tension between unilateralism and multilateralism in US foreign policy. It would be superficial to associate this with the administration of the younger Bush, even though his National Security Assistant, Condeleezza Rice, predicted that it would 'proceed from the firm ground of the national interest, not from the interests of an illusory international community'.[81] This certainly reflected a change of rhetoric compared to the Clinton administration, yet it was Clinton's Secretary of State Madeleine Albright who defended the use of cruise missiles against Iraq in February 1998 with supreme arrogance: 'If we have to use force, it is because we are America. We are the indispensable nation. We stand tall. We see farther into the future.'[82] Huntington cites the bombing of Iraq as one in a long list of unilateral actions taken by the US under Clinton. He comments: 'In acting as if this were a unipolar world, the United States is also becoming increasingly alone in the world . . . While the United States regularly denounces various countries as "rogue states", in the eyes of many countries it is becoming the rogue superpower.'[83]

The tension between unilateralism and multilateralism is a structural one. The US is dependent on other states to achieve its objectives and indeed sometimes shares common interests with them, but it is not merely the tool of 'collective capital' (as Hardt and Negri assert), since it both has distinct interests of its own and a greater capacity than other states to pursue them. This is true at the economic level, where the US must deal with other major constellations of capitalist interests such as the EU and Japan, but it is also true at the geopolitical level. The strategic position of the US is in many cases comparable to that of Britain a century ago. It is a vast continental island offshore the Eurasian landmass where the bulk of the world's productive resources are concentrated. Its main military advantage lies in naval and air supremacy, reflected in the role of the carrier battle groups on which Kennedy lavishes such praise, and sustained by a worldwide network of bases. The relatively small professional Army and Marine Corps are too valuable to risk high casualties (still in any case politically very sensitive nearly a generation after the fall of Saigon). As has been forcefully argued by Zbigniew Brzezinski (National Security Assistant in the Carter Administration), US dominance of the Eurasian landmass depends critically on building up long- and short-term coalitions and keeping potential adversaries divided and isolated.[84] But American overconfidence and the perception that the compromises required for coalition-building are too costly to US interests sometimes lead to violent unilateralist lurches on Washington's part. Thus the Pentagon chafed at the restrictions imposed by NATO's cumbersome decision-making procedures during the 1999 Balkan War.

The Bush administration's response to 9–11 illustrates all these tensions.[85] The immediate military objective of attacking and destroying the Taliban and al-Qaeda in their Afghan strongholds served two larger purposes: to eliminate an urgent physical threat to the continental US and to demonstrate to the world (including potential geopolitical challengers such as Russia and China) the high price of any attack on American power and interests. Pursuing this objective necessitated the construction of an extensive coalition – in part thanks to the imperative to gain physical access to Afghanistan through the cooperation of Pakistan, the Taliban's sponsor, and of Russia, still the dominant power in Central Asia. But the faction in the Bush administration that wanted to subordinate coalition-building to the priorities of a global war directed from Washington rapidly won out. NATO, which had invoked for the first time in its history Article 5 of the North Atlantic Treaty, declaring the attacks on the US one on all its member states, was snubbed. Offers of military help even from relatively close Western allies were unceremoniously spurned: the war in Afghanistan had to be won by *American* arms, as a reassertion of *American* power. In the course of the war, US bases spread throughout Central Asia: greater American access to a region with vast energy reserves was not, as many conspiracy theorists argued, the hidden purpose of the attack on Afghanistan, but it certainly was a substantial incidental benefit.

Most important, however, was the substantial extension of war aims expressed by George W. Bush in his State of the Union address on 29 January 2002. Reaffirming that 'our war on terror is just beginning', Bush announced that, in addition to directly attacking terrorist networks, '[o]ur second goal is to prevent regimes that sponsor terror from threatening America or our friends and allies with weapons of mass destruction', and named Iran, Iraq, and North Korea as 'an axis of evil'.[86] Under-Secretary of State John Bolton subsequently extended the net, identifying Libya, Syria, and Cuba as 'state sponsors of terrorism that are pursuing or who have the potential to pursue weapons of mass destruction'.[87] This developing 'Bush Doctrine' conjured up the prospect of a permanent state of global war. According to Nicholas Lemann, 'all the indications are that Bush is going to use September 11th as the occasion to launch a new, aggressive American foreign policy that would represent a broad change in direction rather than a specific war on terrorism.' He traced this policy's origins to a strategy document authorized by Vice-President Dick Cheney when he was the elder Bush's Defense Secretary in the early 1990s, the nub of which was summed up by one of Cheney's advisers thus: 'it is a vital US interest to be willing to use force if necessary' in order to 'preclude the rise of another global rival for the indefinite future'.[88]

In other words, the leading forces inside the Bush administration have seized the opportunity provided by 11 September to use their enormous military advantage to consolidate America's position as the dominant global power. Military action will be taken probably against Iraq and possibly against other countries deemed to be 'rogue states', more because of their recalcitrance than in punishment of their violations of human rights or international law (other states closely aligned to Washington such as Israel and Pakistan are allowed to commit comparable crimes with impunity). Making an example of a few outlaws would send a signal to all the other powers. Meanwhile, US forces spread across the globe. The *Guardian* reported in early 2002:

> Today, almost six months after the attacks on New York and Washington, the US is putting in place a network of forward bases stretching from the Middle East across the entire length of Asia, from the Red Sea to the Pacific.
>
> US forces are active in the biggest array of countries since the Second World War. Troops, sailors and airmen are now established in countries where they have never before had a presence. The aim is to provide platforms from which to launch attacks on any group perceived by George Bush to be a danger to the US.[89]

The truly fearful implications of the Bush administration's strategic planning were revealed when details of its

Nuclear Posture Review were leaked soon after the 'axis of evil' speech. This document listed Russia, China, North Korea, Iraq, Iran, Syria, and Libya as potential nuclear adversaries, and proposed the integration of nuclear and conventional capabilities – for example, the addition of nuclear warheads to 'bunker buster' weapons intended to kill enemy leaders such as Saddam Hussein.[90] Such Strangelovian plans are not merely an eccentricity of the current administration. In February 1997 US Space Command announced its objective of 'Full Spectrum Dominance' – i.e. American military superiority on land, sea, air, and space, explaining: 'Although unlikely to be challenged by a global peer competitor, the United States will continue to be challenged regionally. The globalization of the world economy will also continue, with a widening between "haves" and "have-nots".' The document proceeds to outline the respects in which 'space superiority is emerging as an essential element of battlefield success and future warfare'.[91]

This rather naïve juxtaposition of high-tech warfare and socio-economic trends reveals something fundamental about the contemporary world. The response of the Bush administration to 11 September – to declare a permanent state of war implicitly directed against potential as well as actual adversaries – indicates the anxieties at work even at the top of the greatest power in history. The US is at once general guardian of the capitalist system and a fierce participant in global economic and geopolitical competition. Its rulers feel threatened by petty recalcitrants such as Iraq that to some degree function as metonyms for much more serious potential challengers such as China. They also fear the 'have-nots' whose numbers are being swelled by neoliberal policies. These anxieties reflect the logic of capital, a system that, as I have tried to show, is based on exploitation and driven by a blind process of competitive accumulation. Now we see that this process embraces the geopolitical rivalries among states, and that the assertion of military power also is caught up in the same logic.

Capitalism thus is also imperialism: it comes armed to the teeth against external rivals and domestic rivals. Its armoury is growing – indeed the probability that the US or some other power will use nuclear weapons in the next few years has increased.[92] Extending our analysis to include the state system is therefore hardly reassuring. The world is becoming a more frightening place, and the source of this, as of other problems, is capitalism. Perhaps in the comparatively short geopolitical term as well as the longer ecological term, it threatens the planet. What do we do about it?

Summary

- Neo-liberalism has failed even to restore the rates of economic growth that the world enjoyed during the Long Boom of the 1950s and 1960s, let alone to reduce poverty and inequality;
- Although financial markets provide the most visible evidence of the irrationality and inhumanity of liberal capitalism, they are more a symptom than the fundamental source of the problem;
- Capitalism is best understood along the lines pioneered by Marx, as a system based on the exploitation of wage-labour and driven by the competitive accumulation of capital;
- The process of competitive accumulation is responsible for capitalism's chronic tendency towards crises of over-investment and profitability: financial speculation feeds this tendency but is not its primary cause;
- The competitive struggle among the multinational corporations that dominate the contemporary world economy is also the main driving force behind the processes of environmental destruction that threaten the life of humankind along with that of many other species;

- Capitalist competition takes the form not merely of economic rivalries between firms but also of geo-political conflicts among states: the current efforts of American imperialism to assert its primacy over the other Great Powers threatens the world with a new era of wars, with incalculable consequences;
- The major problems facing humankind – poverty, social injustice, economic instability, environmental destruction, and war – have the same source, in the capitalist system: the solution to these problems must, accordingly, be a radical one.

– 2 –
Varieties and Strategies

Varieties of anti-capitalism

The movement against global capitalism is very far from being homogeneous. Indeed, it prides itself in its diversity and capacity to contain an immense variety of differences. This is undeniably a source of strength in many ways: numerous commentators have registered the colourful array of forces represented on great mobilizations such as those at Seattle, Genoa, Porto Alegre, and Barcelona – trade unionists and crusties, revolutionary socialists and autonomists, NGO activists and Communists, nationalists and Third Worldists, peace campaigners and the Black Bloc, along with vast numbers of young people representing all the variety of culture and lifestyle that their generation embraces. Implicit in all this are several distinct political approaches to the issues of strategy and principle that face the anti-capitalist movement. It may therefore be useful, before directly discussing some of these issues, briefly to consider some of the main political approaches that fall under the rubric of anti-capitalism. The list that follows is far from exhaustive; moreover, though I have sought to avoid caricature, I may not always have succeeded. It is also important to note that, since the realities of ideology and politics are always complicated, individuals and organizations may in reality fall under more than one of the positions listed below.

(i) Reactionary anti-capitalism

Since the onset of industrial capitalism in the late nineteenth century, many have responded by rejecting this social system in the name of some earlier state of affairs. Georg Lukács named this 'Romantic anti-capitalism'.[1] This ideological formation is a complex one: often nostalgia for an idealized past has helped to motivate the struggle to achieve a new society that does not simply reject modernity – in the British socialist tradition William Morris's evolution from the Pre-Raphaelites to revolutionary Marxism is a case in point. In the same spirit, Brazilian artists demonstrated at Porto Alegre II under a banner bearing the slogan 'Re-enchant the World!' But a critique of capitalism from the standpoint of an organic premodern order has also been one of the main ideological impulses behind the extreme right. In an important study of pre-war French fascism Zeev Sternhell sums up fascist ideology as 'a synthesis of organic nationalism and of anti-Marxist socialism, a revolutionary ideology founded on the refusal at once of liberalism, of Marxism, and of democracy'. Its aim was

> a communitarian and anti-individualist civilization, alone capable of assuring the survival of a human collectivity where all the strata and all the classes of society would be perfectly integrated. The natural framework of this harmonious, organic collectivity is the Nation. A nation purged and revitalized, where the individual is only a cell of a collective organism; a nation rejoicing in a moral unity that liberalism and Marxism, both factors of dissociation and of war, could never assure it.[2]

This kind of reactionary response to capitalism is still, alas, very much with us. The threat represented by contemporary European fascist movements was underlined by Jean-Marie Le Pen's success in driving the Socialist Party Prime Minister, Lionel Jospin, into third place in the first round of the French presidential elections in April 2002. Reactionary anti-capitalism is alive also in the opposition to economic globalization by the American far-right, which was especially vocal against the negotiation and ratification of the North American Free Trade Agreement in 1992–3 and to the Uruguay Round of international trade talks that led to the establishment of the World Trade Organization in 1995. In his interesting study of this movement Mark Rupert writes:

> Far-right ideologies of American exceptionalism represent transnational integration as an insidious threat to the special identity of America as a (white, masculine, Christian) nation. In such ways Americanist ideologies authorize resistance to globalization as well as scapegoating and encouraging hostility to those seen as outside of, different, or dissenting from their visions of national identity.[3]

Since the contemporary anti-capitalist movement emerged in North America also out of opposition to NAFTA and the WTO, some of its enemies sought to smear it by association with the anti-globalization far-right. This is hardly plausible: one of the movement's main impulses is internationalism and, in particular, solidarity with the poor and oppressed of the South. Moreover, the kind of critique of capitalism that it has developed is, as the previous chapter sought to illustrate, a structural one directed at the logic of the *system*; by contrast, the American far-right rely on a version of the classic fascist conspiracy theory, according to which a clique of (naturally mainly Jewish) international financiers have successfully manipulated the global political economy in order to construct a 'New World Order' under their domination.

Rupert notes: 'As a consequence of this agent-centred world-view, Patriots are unable to envision, explain, or critique the interrelated structures and processes which left progressives see at work in the nexus between the US and the global economy.'[4]

The conspiratorial explanations employed by the far-right indicate the limited and superficial sense in which their ideologies can be called anti-capitalist. Sternhell observes that, 'if fascist ideology sought the victory of spirit and will over matter, it attacked bourgeois society and its "materialist" values but not capitalism, or private property'.[5] Similarly Henry Ashby Turner writes of Hitler: 'His commitment to economic competition and private property derived not from expediency but rather from his fanatically Social Darwinist beliefs about the nature of mankind and human society . . . Hitler was an anti-socialist out of conviction, not out of opportunism.'[6] The Nazis' pseudo-revolutionary denunciations of 'Jewish finance capital' allowed them to build a mass movement; their anti-Marxism made them acceptable (if suspect) allies for German elites. The National Socialist regime involved a conflictual partnership with big capital, in which the revolutionary impulses it had mobilized, denied social realization, were displaced onto the extermination of a racialized enemy.[7] Similar processes of displacement are evidently at work in contemporary European fascist movements and in the American anti-globalization right. Though these are, as yet, fortunately acted out on a much smaller stage than pre-war Germany, the existence of a far-right critique of capitalist globalization is a portent of what might develop if more universalist and authentically radical challenges fail.

(ii) Bourgeois anti-capitalism

This might seem like a null category, indeed the expression of a contradiction in terms. But ideologies do not obey the law of non-contradiction. Marx in the *Communist Mani-*

festo sardonically diagnoses the case of 'Conservative or Bourgeois Socialism' whose proponents 'want all the advantages of modern social conditions without the struggles and dangers necessarily resulting therefrom. They desire the existing state of society minus its revolutionary and disintegrating elements.'[8] There are counterparts of this kind of attitude in the contemporary anti-capitalist movement. Noreena Hertz is a case in point. 'My argument is not intended to be anti-capitalist', she writes, going on to make the assertion criticized at the beginning of the previous chapter: 'Capitalism is clearly the best system for generating wealth, and free trade and open capital markets have brought unprecedented growth to most if not all of the world.'[9] Yet Hertz has been careful, through a skilful media campaign, to associate herself with the movement against corporate globalization, attending the protests at Prague and Genoa, and boasting of the 'anti-capitalist' Boudicca trouser suit she wore as a member of the 'progressive grouping' at the pro-business World Economic Forum in New York.[10]

Plainly anti-capitalism needs its own Tom Wolfe to anatomize the contemporary forms of radical chic. But Hertz is representative of a wider viewpoint. Her complaint with capitalism is not that it exists, but that it has become too powerful:

> Over the past two decades the balance of power between politics and commerce has shifted radically, leaving politicians increasingly subordinate to the colossal power of big business ... And, as business has extended its role, it has ... actually come to define the corporate public realm. The corporate state has come to define the political state.[11]

Hertz's remedy is, naturally enough, to correct this imbalance. Indeed, corporations are themselves stepping in to fill the vacuum left by abdicating politicians. She tells us that 'business is now in many ways better placed than any other institution to act as the primary agent of justice in much of the developing world', and welcomes the privatization of welfare as 'an attractive development', if 'managed correctly'. But more grassroots initiatives are also necessary to put pressure on corporations and governments to live up to their responsibilities. Hertz stresses the beneficial effects of consumer activism, but is more ambivalent about direct action: 'Protest acts as a countervailing force to the Silent Takeover, yet because it is not fully inclusive it shares the illegitimacy of its opponent ... The silent majority risks being disempowered by the vocal minority.' Indeed, rising voter apathy – itself largely a product of the declining power of elected governments – could culminate in 'the end of politics itself – the takeover of politics by protest'.[12]

The issue of whether or not protests are inclusive is a real enough problem, and one to which I return below. That aside, Hertz's critique is highly derivative, and of interest only for two reasons. First, it illustrates in particularly pure form the tendency of critics of corporate globalization to accept one of the main theses of its cruder boosters – namely that greater international integration has deprived nation-states of any power to influence economic developments. It cannot be repeated often enough that this thesis is both false and dangerously misleading.[13] Second, Hertz undoubtedly articulates the spontaneous ideology of a spectrum of business opinion. This includes, for example, the growing Corporate Social Responsibility (CSR) industry, a phenomenon that is itself to some degree a response to protest. The *Observer* noted: 'Company chairmen forced to cower behind police lines cannot help but be impressed by the strength of feeling and powers of organization of people who might be ignored if they contented themselves with polite protest.'[14] The Global Compact launched by the United Nations Secretary General, Kofi Annan, together with some leading multinational corporations represents a similar effort to bring together big business and 'civil society'. The *Financial Times* cynically exposed the real reasons why chief executives love CSR. Clearly, they do not dare risk damaging their brands by being seen as hostile to people or the planet. But, just as importantly, CSR gives them the opportunity to imbue their brands with positive, popular values that plug into concerns for the environment and human rights. The beauty of it is that, compared with the cost of trying to build the same brand attributes through advertising and public relations, it probably works out rather cheap.[15]

Like the efforts of the IMF and the World Bank to develop a dialogue with their critics, initiatives such as CSR represent a pragmatic response to external pressures. But some capitalists sincerely support the movement against corporate globalization. For example, the Ruckus Society, which trains activists in the techniques of civil disobedience, received $100,000 from Unilever in 2001. This reflected, not the conversion of a leading multi-national to anti-capitalism, but the terms under which Unilever took over Ben & Jerry's ice-cream business: the corporation agreed to give $5 million to Ben & Jerry's Foundation (from which Global Exchange, one of the key activist coalitions, received $1 million over three years) and to donate at least $1.1 million a year to 'social change groups'. According to Ben Cohen, one of the two founders of Ben & Jerry's, during the takeover negotiations, '[w]e explained to Unilever that the values of Ben & Jerry's would be anti-globalization and they said they were very much supporters of globalization.' It would have been fun to be a fly on the wall at these meetings. Ben and Jerry are not the only '60s generation capitalists to back the movement. According to James Harding, Anita Roddick, founder of Body Shop and a board member of the Ruckus Society, 'is looking forward to increasing support for anti-sweatshop activists, independent media organizations, dissent groups, and local environmental start-ups, socially responsible ventures and a range of others'.[16]

(iii) Localist anti-capitalism

The intentions of these business sympathizers with the anti-capitalist movement are no doubt sincere and honourable. But their stance does raise the question that runs through this entire book: are certain values plausibly espoused by the movement – in the next chapter I argue that these include, at the minimum, justice, efficiency, democracy, and sustainability – consistent with *any* version of capitalism? This question arises in a more interesting way with respect to the cluster of attitudes that, for want of a better name, I call 'localist anti-capitalism'. By this I mean those activists and intellectuals who advocate, to remedy the ills of contemporary capitalism, a reformed and decentralized market economy. This includes supporters of fair trade – among which Global Exchange, one of the driving forces behind the Seattle protests, figures prominently – and also many variants of Green thought.

Fair trade is essentially the idea that consumers in the North should organize to promote more equitable trade relationships with producers in the South. Deborah James of Global Exchange writes:

> Fair Trade means an equitable and fair partnership between marketers in North America and producer groups in Asia, Africa, Latin America, and other parts of the world. Fair Traders agree to abide by the following criteria:
> * Paying a fair wage in the local context;
> * Offering employees opportunities for advancement;
> * Providing equal opportunities for all people;
> * Engaging in environmentally sustainable practices;
> * Being open to public accountability;
> * Building long-term trade relationships;
> * Providing healthy and safe working conditions within the local context;
> * Providing financial and technical assistance to producers wherever possible.[17]

Fair trade is localist in the sense that it seeks justice, not (at least in the first instance) in system transformation, but rather in the development of fair micro-relationships among a series of market actors starting with the immediate producers through an alternative distribution system to the socially aware consumer. But this approach admits without too much difficulty of extension to a systemic alternative to global capitalism. Colin Hines has offered an account of what this alternative, which he calls 'localization', might look like:

> Everything that could be produced within a nation or region should be. Long-distance trade is then reduced to supplying what could not come from within one country or geographical grouping of countries. This would allow an increase in local control of the economy and the potential for it being shared out more fairly, locally. Technology and information would be encouraged to flow, when and where they could strengthen local economies. Under these circumstances, beggar-your-neighbour globalization gives way to the potentially more cooperative better-your-neighbour localization.[18]

Hines's aim is to redirect power as far as possible towards small-scale communities. As such, it dovetails in with the aims of the Green movement, as well as with the critique offered by another British anti-corporate campaigner and writer, George Monbiot.[19] But the programme that Hines seeks to develop is robustly interventionist. The power of the nation-state and larger regional groupings would be deployed to ensure that 'capital remains predominantly where it is generated in order to fund sustainable development and create jobs', tariffs would discriminate in favour of domestic goods, other steps would be taken to dismantle the multinationals and promote small and medium enterprises, and the introduction of resource taxation would protect the environment and promote job creation.[20]

In many ways localism is reminiscent of the thinking of the nineteenth-century French socialist Pierre Joseph Proudhon, who believed that the concentration of economic power, particularly in the banking system, prevented the laws of the market from operating properly; measures to reduce this concentration and restore power to small producers – artisans and peasants – would set the market economy to rights and thereby achieve social justice. This solution attracted much scornful criticism from Marx, who commented on the Proudhonist proposal to abolish money but maintain an economy based on the production and exchange of commodities: 'One might just as well abolish the Pope while leaving Catholicism in existence.'[21] There is a definitely Proudhonian ring to Hines's conclusion: 'Localization Will Bale Out the Market'.[22] Whether one can in this fashion distinguish between the good and bad sides of the market is one of the main issues addressed in the next chapter.

(iv) Reformist anti-capitalism

One of the merits of Hines's argument for localization is that it brings out into the open the issue of the nation-state. The state is generally seen as one of the main victims of economic globalization: does it follow that it is a potential ally of the anti-capitalist movement? Hines answers this question in the affirmative. Even greater stress is laid on the nation-state as an agent of desirable social transformation by those who advocate, as an alternative to neo-liberalism, the return to a more regulated capitalism. It is this position that I have chosen to call 'reformist anti-capitalism'. In the classical labour movement 'reformism' referred to the strategy of social democracy of achieving socialism by parliamentary means. Few contemporary social democrats believe that a socialist alternative to capitalism is any longer feasible. Instead they seek to regulate and humanize capitalism. Reformist anti-capitalists differ from localists in the sense that they focus on the national and the international levels as the main fields of action.

It is in fact begging an important question to describe the aim of this variant of anti-capitalism as a *return* to a more regulated capitalism. This accurately captures the aim of important strands of the reformist wing of the movement. Patrick Bond argues that within what he calls the 'New Social Movements' who seek 'to promote the globalization of people and halt or at a minimum radically modify the globalization of capital' there is

> an ongoing debate over whether energy should be invested in helping Post-Washington Consensus reforms constitute a global state regulatory capacity – expanding upon embryos like the IMF and World Bank, WTO, United Nations and BIS – or whether in contrast the immediate task should be defunding and denuding the legitimacy of the current sites of international regulation so as to reconstitute progressive politics on the national scale.[23]

As we have seen, James Tobin proposed his famous tax on foreign exchange transactions in part 'to preserve and promote autonomy of national macroeconomic and monetary policies'.[24] Bernard Cassen, until recently the President of ATTAC, which campaigns for the Tobin Tax, and the editorial team of the hugely influential monthly *Le Monde diplomatique* are close politically to Jean-Pierre Chevènement, leader of the Mouvement des Citoyens and advocate of *souverainisme*, the restoration of national sovereignty. Another key anti-capitalist leader, Walden Bello, the Director of Focus on the Global South, explicitly advocates the abolition of the WTO and the other international financial institutions in order to return to a version of the Bretton Woods System:

> It was under such a relatively pluralistic global system, where hegemonic power was still far from institutionalized in a set of all-encompassing and powerful multilateral organizations that the Latin American countries and many

Asian countries were able to achieve a modicum of industrial development in the period from 1960–70. It was under
a more pluralistic system, under a GATT that was limited in
its power, flexible and more sympathetic to the special
status of developing countries, that East and South-East
Asian countries were able to become newly industrializing
countries through activist state trade and industrial policies
that departed significantly from the free-market biases
enshrined in the WTO . . . It is in such a fluid, less struc-
tured, more pluralistic world, with multiple checks and bal-
ances that the nations and communities of the South will be
able to carve out the space to develop based on their values,
their rhythms, and the strategies of their choice.[25]

But no one in the movement seeks simply such a world
of relatively autonomous national capitalisms. For one
thing, the Tobin Tax can only be implemented on an international (though not a universal) scale. The most detailed
study of the tax, by Heikki Patomäki, a scholar involved
in ATTAC, suggests that it could be initiated by as few as
thirty states, provided that they covered at least 20 per cent
of the foreign exchange market, and envisages the development of a Tobin Tax Organization that would even-
tually become a universal institution subordinated to a
reformed United Nations.[26] Rather like Tobin, Kamal Malhotra advocates the establishment of a World Financial
Authority in order to achieve 'the subordination of
the global level of governance to the local, national and
regional levels – but especially the national'.[27] A reformed
European Union is often seen as an agent of the desired
regulation. But it is not simply that the regulation of financial markets requires international action: most supporters of the Tobin Tax do not envisage its revenues staying
in the advanced economies where most currency transactions take place, but rather advocate their redistribution
from North to South. One of the main impulses behind
the anti-capitalist movement, and one that unites all its
different wings, is the desire to remedy global injustice. It
seems quite unimaginable that this desire can be fulfilled

simply by promoting autonomous national development, since this would leave people vulnerable to all the contingencies that derive from history and geography, not to speak of the injustices that nation-states have shown themselves all too capable of committing.

Susan George, Vice-President of ATTAC and a long-standing champion of the Third World, accordingly proposes a 'new, updated and Keynesian strategy . . . , not just for the United States or in Europe but throughout the world. We need vast injections of crisis-directed resources into the global economy. They must be linked to environmental renewal, poverty eradication, and democratic governance.' She envisages this 'Planetary Contract' being administered by a new international institution and financed by such measures as the Tobin Tax and a Unitary Profits Tax on transnational corporations.[28] Proposals for an international debtors' cartel willing to threaten and perhaps to implement the repudiation of Third World debt as a means of pressure on the G7, the international financial institutions, and the big Northern banks are in much the same spirit, and could be seen as a way of achieving such a global Keynesianism.[29]

The obverse of this attempt to rebuild at the global level a version of the more humane and regulated capitalism that flourished (at least in the North) at the national level during the 1970s is a rejection of revolution. Once again, this has been most clearly articulated by George:

> I regret that I must confess that I no longer know what 'overthrowing capitalism' means at the beginning of the twenty-first century. Perhaps we are going to witness what the philosopher Paul Virilio has called 'the global accident'. If it happens, it will certainly be accompanied by immense human suffering. If all the financial markets and all the stock exchanges collapsed at the same time, millions of people would find themselves back on the dole, bank failures would massively exceed the capacity of governments to prevent catastrophes, insecurity and crime would become the norm and we would be plunged into the

Hobbesian hell of the war of all against all. Call me a 'reformist' if you like, but I don't want such a future any more than the neo-liberal future.[30]

(v) Autonomist anti-capitalism

If the reformist wing of the movement against capitalist globalization is characterized by its commitment to the nation-state, acting alone or in concert, as a means of taming the market, autonomism by contrast distinguishes itself by a renunciation of centralized power and a pre-occupation with the movement's distinctive methods of organizing and acting. I have given this band of opinion the name 'autonomism' because one of its main sources lies in the coalition of Italian far-left groupings that first popularized the term in the 1970s. Toni Negri, co-author of *Empire*, is the best-known theorist of Italian autonomism.[31] The vocabulary of *Empire* impregnates the rhetoric of the celebrated Italian activist coalition known, after the white overalls they used to cover the body armour they wore on demonstrations, as the *tute bianche*, or, since Genoa, as the *disobbedienti*. The *tute bianche* have exerted a worldwide influence. But autonomism draws its strength even more from the distinctive style developed by the anti-capitalist movement as it first developed in North America – that of decentralized 'coalition of coalitions', as Kevin Danaher of Global Exchange put it, organizing the protests on the basis of consensus through a variety of different methods such as the affinity group, the spokes-council, the convergence centre, and Indy-media.[32]

More than anyone else Naomi Klein has emerged as the great exponent of this activist style as a new form of radical politics:

> The fact that these campaigns are so decentralized is not a source of incoherence and fragmentation. Rather, it is a reasonable, even ingenious adaptation both to pre-existing fragmentation within progressive networks and to changes in the broader culture. It is a by-product of the explosion

of NGOs, which, since the Rio Summit in 1992, have been gaining power and prominence. There are so many NGOs involved in anti-corporate campaigns that nothing but the hub and spokes model could possibly accommodate their different styles, tactics and goals . . . One of the great strengths of this model of laissez-faire organizing is that it has proven extraordinarily difficult to control, largely because it is so different from the organizing principles of the institutions and corporations it targets. It responds to corporate concentration with a maze of fragmentation, to globalization with its own kind of localization, to power consolidation with radical power dispersal . . . A US military report on the Zapatista rising in Chiapas even got in on the game. According to a study produced by RAND, the Zapatistas were waging 'a war of the flea' that, thanks to the Internet and the global NGO network, turned into 'a war of the swarm'. The military challenge of a war of the swarm, the researchers noted, is that it has no 'central leadership or command structure; it is multi-headed, impossible to decapitate'.[33]

As this passage indicates, the Zapatista movement has been one of the main reference-points for autonomist anti-capitalists (indeed the main grouping associated with the *tute bianche* called themselves *Ya Basta!*, after the Zapatista slogan: 'Enough is enough!'). The Zapatista Army of National Liberation (EZLN)'s initial manifesto called for a march on the capital. But – perhaps because their forces were soon surrounded and contained by the Mexican military, so that the EZLN's survival came to depend on the solidarity they could evoke in the rest of Mexico and the world – their programme came to focus primarily on demands for the recognition of the collective rights of Mexico's indigenous people as part of the more general democratization of what was, until the 2000 presidential elections, a one-party state.[34] Marcos has theorized this apparent retreat, suggesting: 'Perhaps, for example, the new political morality will be constructed in a new space that will not require the taking or retention of power, but the counterweight and opposition that contains and obliges the power to "rule by obeying".'[35]

At the same time, however, Marcos sometimes sounds like the *souverainistes* of ATTAC and *Le Monde diplomatique*: 'The Zapatistas believe that in Mexico recovery and defence of national sovereignty are part of the anti-liberal revolution . . . it is necessary to defend the state in the face of globalization'.[36] This contrasts very strongly with the argument of that other key autonomist reference-point, *Empire*. Here Negri and his collaborator Michael Hardt argue not simply that national sovereignty is being irrevocably displaced by imperial sovereignty, but that even at its most progressive, in the movements for colonial liberation, nationalism tended to repress the difference inherent in the 'multitude' – the exploited antithesis to capital – in order to constitute a homogeneous 'people' as an imaginary counterpart to the nation-state. 'The deterritorializing desire of the multitude is the motor that drives the entire process of capitalist development, and capital must constantly attempt to contain it.'[37] Thus Hardt along with other autonomists declares: 'The Empire is the enemy of the multitude, but this does not mean that the old nation states are our friends.'[38]

Apparent contradictions of this kind are rarely confronted by autonomist intellectuals, partly because they tend to favour the allusive, metaphorical language of which Marcos is such a master. Klein, for example, having popularized the idea of the anti-capitalist movement as a decentralized 'swarm', more recently borrowed another metaphor from Luca Casarini, one of the main leaders of the Italian *disobbedienti*, at the second World Social Forum:

> 'It's about – how do you say it English? – this,' he said. And using the forum's activist Esperanto of butchered second languages and mime, he tugged at his T-shirt sleeve and showed me the seam.
>
> Right, the seams. Maybe change isn't really about what is said and done in the centres. It's about the seams, the in-between spaces with their hidden strength.[39]

The proliferation of metaphors that celebrate decentralized forms of organizing isn't necessarily particularly helpful in clarifying the strategy implied by this discourse. Hardt's and Negri's concept of the multitude has been widely taken up, but it seems more like an avowal of good intentions than a serious analytical concept. At Porto Alegre II, Hardt more or less admitted this, calling it 'a political concept' that was 'not about what is, but about what could be'. It was 'intended to demonstrate that class concepts need not choose between unity and plurality'. Hardt described the multitude as 'singularities that act in common'. He said that the concept embraced 'all those who work under the rule of capital', and that it was 'analogous to the classical Marxist concept of the proletariat, but without the narrowing down that happened to that concept in the nineteenth and twentieth centuries'.[40] One political function of the idea of the multitude is to demarcate the autonomists from the classical left. After Porto Alegre II, Casarini, Hardt, and others issued a text denouncing 'the bourgeois left and the white-skinned worker socialism of European origins' and celebrating the Argentinian rising of December 2001 as a vindication of their alternative approach:

> it is the work of the multitude that appears as the only constituent principle. Far from being a problem, the fragmentation of the working class and of its union representatives constitutes the condition for the affirmation of a social multiplicity capable to [sic] ignite the crisis of the state (including its armed forces) as it can transform the failure of the democracy of financial techniques into an unprecedented process of radical democracy.[41]

(vi) Socialist anti-capitalism

For most of the twentieth century socialism and anti-capitalism were largely co-extensive categories. That this is no longer the case is a consequence of the long crisis of

the left that began with the reflux of the post-1968 movements in the mid-1970s but was hugely reinforced by the
collapse of the Stalinist system in 1989–91. Even the anti-
Stalinist left was weakened by the disappearance of the
principal regime that appeared to embody an alternative,
however bureaucratic and corrupt, to market capitalism.
The distinctive character of the contemporary anti-
capitalist movement reflects its emergence in an ideological climate defined by the apparent triumph of liberal
capitalism and eclipse of Marxism. This was particularly
pronounced in the United States, where the organized left
had been relatively marginal throughout the twentieth
century. In Europe, however, the movement developed in
a significantly different context. Though weakened by the
neo-liberal offensive and the post-1989 ideological crisis,
both the labour movement and substantial organizations
of the reformist and revolutionary left survived. Given the
eclipse of Stalinism and the rightward evolution of social
democracy, the idea of a socialist alternative to capitalism
has to a large extent devolved onto the revolutionary left
and, more particularly, on movements in the Trotskyist
tradition, especially in Western Europe.

While some Trotskyist tendencies reacted to the emergence of the anti-capitalist movement in a characteri-
stically dogmatic and sectarian fashion, the two main
international Trotskyist currents, the Fourth International
(FI) and the International Socialist Tendency (IST), quickly
recognized the potential of the movement.[42] Activists of
the FI's leading European organization, the Ligue Com-
muniste Révolutionnaire, performed an important role in
ATTAC from the start; supporters of the FI from both
Latin America and Europe have been heavily involved in
the World Social Forums at Porto Alegre. Meanwhile the
three biggest European affiliates of the IST, the Socialist
Workers Parties in Britain, Ireland, and Greece, have been
playing a major part in the development of the movement
in these countries. In Italy, however, a socialist version
of anti-capitalism has been taken up by a much more

substantial organization, the Partito della Rifondazione Comunista (PRC). Founded by the minority that rejected the transformation of the old Communist Party into a Third Way formation, the Left Democrats, the PRC managed to avoid decline into a Stalinist rump, and maintained itself as a mass party with parliamentary representation and a substantial trade-union following. In the summer of 2001, the PRC mobilized heavily for the Genoa protests and both participated in and benefited from the subsequent radicalization. Its leader, Fausto Bertinotti, made clear the PRC's support for the movement against neo-liberalism and war.

But if these and other socialist organizations have strongly identified with the anti-capitalist movement and taken part, sometimes prominently, in its protests, they remain very much a minority force. The idea that socialism is the alternative to capitalism has as yet little currency in the movement, in the North at least. Patrick Bond wrote on the eve of Seattle: 'Given the character of the (over-accumulation) crisis, it would indeed be logical to move from a Marxian analysis to a revolutionary socialist strategy. But there is so little organization aiming in this direction that it would be futile.'[43] The socialist voice has grown louder within the movement. At the final meeting of the social movements at Porto Alegre II, the Brazilian Landless Labourers' Movement (MST), whose leadership has a Maoist background, unfurled a banner declaring: 'Another World is Possible – Only as Socialism'. But (despite the ecstatic response this received at the time), this is very far from being the dominant view among anti-capitalists. It is up to socialists to show, often in the face of some hostility from both the more conservative NGOs and the autonomists, that their conception of the world is relevant to this new movement – that socialism is a credible and feasible alternative to capitalism, and that the organized working class still is the decisive agent of social transformation. The rest of this book is, among other things, a contribution to this task.

Reform or revolution?

The anti-capitalist movement is undeniably a new movement. But as it has developed it has begun to confront
some old problems – problems that have in one form or
another faced every great movement for social transformation over the past two centuries. In many respects,
implicit in all these problems is the ancient dilemma of
reform or revolution: is the aim of the movement gradually to humanize the system or completely to replace, and,
if its goal is the latter, can this be achieved without what
Susan George rejects – the forcible overthrow of the main
institutions of capitalist power? In case this might seem
like a diagnosis imposed from without on the movement
in accordance with an out-dated agenda, let us consider
how this question implicitly informs a series of more specific issues.

(1) *Dialogue.* The established powers can respond to
major challenges from below in two ways – repression or
incorporation. In other words, they can seek simply to
crush a movement for change by the use of coercive and
juridical power, or instead to weaken it by making limited
concessions designed to divide the movement, in particular by winning over the more moderate elements and
isolating the radicals. The anti-capitalist movement has
so far faced both responses. The repressive reaction was
most visible in the police violence at Genoa; the anti-
terrorism legislation passed by the United States, Britain,
and other leading states after 11 September represents a
very serious longer-term threat to all those engaging in
direct action. But there have also been efforts by different
sections of what one might broadly call the international
capitalist establishment to draw the movement into
dialogue.

One form that this has taken is the efforts by the International Monetary Fund and the World Bank to develop

discussions with their critics, particularly after the avalanche of attacks that descended on the international financial institutions (IFIs) in the late 1990s. This approach has had no effect in slowing the momentum of the anti-capitalist movement: on the contrary, the debates staged between representatives of global capitalism and of the movement before the IMF/World Bank annual general meeting in Prague in September 2000 and at the first World Social Forum in January 2001 simply fed the movement's sense that their opponents are morally and intellectually bankrupt. Nevertheless, a significant number of the more respectable NGOs were willing to engage in a serious dialogue with the Bank and the IMF over proposals for their reform. Patrick Bond has denounced what he calls 'a terribly dangerous tendency amongst the more conservative ... NGOs and environmental groups – some even derisively call them Co-Opted NGOs or Co-NGOs – to cut pragmatic yet ultimately absurd and untenable deals with the establishment'.[44]

Some go further and denounce 'NGOs in the Service of Imperialism'.[45] One does not have to endorse this sort of blanket condemnation of all NGOs to see that many find themselves in a highly ambiguous position. It is commonplace to conceptualize the NGOs as a key element in 'civil society'. In the liberal democratic discourse that became very fashionable in the 1980s and 1990s this expression is used to refer to social organizations and institutions that occupy a sphere distinct from the state and the economy and therefore have a capacity for independent action.[46] But independent is precisely what many of the NGOs are not. The large-scale privatization of aid in the neo-liberal era transformed the NGOs into agencies for the distribution of state funds. Simultaneously, the relative decline in Western aid budgets has forced many NGOs to compete for private donations, encouraging them to pursue melodramatic media strategies to attract publicity. One outcome of this process was the organization of campaigns by NGOs such as Médecins sans Frontières for Western military intervention to support their operations in Africa and the Balkans.[47]

These complex relationships with Western governments have set distinct limits to the ability of major NGOs to campaign for radical measures to alleviate Third World poverty. The real dependence of many NGOs on the state is illustrated by the skill with which Clare Short, Secretary of State for International Development under Tony Blair, has played the NGOs, sometimes lulling them into acquiescence by telling them what they want to hear about the government's supposed commitment to development, sometimes – when they dare to criticize official policy, as many did over the failure of the G8 summit in Genoa seriously to address Third World poverty and the US bombing campaign against Afghanistan – denouncing them as well-meaning but stupid white liberals.

The IFIs' efforts at dialogue were nevertheless ineffective, mainly because the World Bank in particular offered little more than the same old neo-liberal policies dressed up in the language of 'empowerment'. Renaming structural adjustment programmes 'poverty reduction strategies' is positively Orwellian, since what these do is actually increase poverty, but only those who wanted to be deceived can have been taken in.[48] Walden Bello, probably the anti-capitalist movement's most influential strategic thinker, found ready support for his argument, for example in a paper with Nicola Bullard that a 'crisis of legitimacy now envelops the institutions of global economic governance'. He warned against 'the soft corporate counteroffensive' designed to 'relegitimize globalization'. To counter it required boycotting the efforts to develop a dialogue between the big corporations and 'civil society'. Furthermore, 'the time is ripe to press and build-up a global campaign for decommissioning or neutering' the IFIs and to 'extend the crisis of legitimacy from the multilateral institutions of global governance to the engine of globalization itself: the transnational corporation'.

Campaigners should stress 'the similarity between the mafia and the TNC'.[49]

More sophisticated attempts at incorporation have come from other quarters. The confrontation at Genoa in July 2001 brought divided reactions from the social-democratic parties that then largely dominated the European Union. Predictably enough, the Blair government in Britain was unremitting in its hostility to the protesters. Indeed, the *Financial Times* reported shortly after the summit: 'Mr Blair has told friends that while the events of Genoa were "unacceptable", they might actually prove "helpful" to those fighting for the cause of free trade and economic liberalization.'[50] Blair's plans to launch an ideological assault on the anti-capitalist movement were in the event diverted into his drive after 11 September to act as a worldwide ambassador for the Bush administration and its 'war on terrorism', but his government continued to be one of the most uncritical Western defenders of the Washington Consensus.

The response to Genoa of the French Prime Minister, Lionel Jospin, was very different: 'France denounces the violence by a tiny minority under the pretext of highlighting the evils of globalization; but it is delighted to see the emergence of a citizens' movement at the planetary level which wants a majority of men and women to share the potential benefits of globalization between rich and poor countries.'[51] Jospin's fellow social democrat, the German Chancellor Gerhard Schröder, had adopted the slogan *die neue Mitte* (the new centre) and toyed with Blair's Third Way, but in September 2001 he called for a debate on the 'weak spots' in the international financial markets and 'how we can react to these relatively autonomous speculative financial flows'.[52] The French and German governments followed this up by setting up a high-level working group on controlling international financial markets – a move that the *Financial Times* described as 'a further feather in the cap of the anti-globalization protesters'.[53]

Jospin's courtship of the anti-capitalist movement did not stop after 11 September. A series of meetings took place between ATTAC leaders and members of the Prime Minister's staff, and in November 2001 the French National Assembly passed an amendment supporting the Tobin Tax. Porto Alegre II attracted a flood of French politicians including Chevènement and six of Jospin's ministers. Henri Weber, a former revolutionary of the 1968 generation now close to Laurent Fabius, Finance Minister under Jospin and leader of the Socialist Party right, called the WSF 'a historic social movement, whose articulation with the governing left is fundamental'.[54]

Undoubtedly this official attention reflected the impact of the anti-capitalist movement. Nevertheless, it did not represent any serious intention on the part of the leaders of European social democracy to change course. Despite the care with which Jospin sought initially to cultivate a socialist image, his 'plural left' government pursued neoliberal policies with considerably greater success than its conservative predecessor. As Philip H. Gordon of the Brookings Institution points out, 'Jospin, as the head of a Socialist-Communist-Green coalition supposedly sympathetic to a statist economy, has actually privatized FFr 240bn worth (€36.4bn, £22.5bn) of state enterprises, more than the past six French governments combined.'[55] It is easy to understand why both Jospin and Schröder should have sought to draw closer to a movement that had demonstrated its capacity to mobilize mass support in the lead-up to hotly contested elections in both France and Germany. Setbacks such as Jospin's humiliating defeat in the 2002 presidential elections make it likely that some European social democrats will make even more strenuous efforts to associate themselves with the anti-globalization cause. The danger for the movement, however, is that in the process it will find that its teeth have been drawn.

(2) *Violence and the state.* The other establishment response – repression – also poses difficulties for the anti-

capitalist movement. As we have seen, especially among the autonomists, it has become commonplace to celebrate the dispersed, fragmented structure of the 'movement of movements' as a strategic virtue that allows it to outflank the centralized power of its opponents. Naomi Klein approvingly quoted Maude Barlow of the Council of Canadians: 'We are up against a boulder. We can't remove it so we try to go underneath it, to go around it and over it.'[56] But what happens if the boulder – in the shape of the capitalist state – doesn't meekly stand there and allow its opponents to walk round it? What if it goes out to get them? One of the most dramatic episodes in the Genoa protests came on 20 July 2001, when different groups took direct action around the city. The *tute bianche*, who specialize in non-violent street tactics, had declared war on the G8 and promised to break into the fenced-off Red Zone where the summit was meeting. Their contingent, based at the Carlini stadium, was ambushed by massed forces of heavily armed *carabinieri*. It was during the ensuing street fighting that Carlo Giuliani was shot dead by the riot police. Interviewed shortly afterwards, the *tute bianche* leader Luca Casarini said:

> The police charged violently. We fought back and I stand by our response as a political fact. Nonetheless, for us to also take up militaristic tactics would be crazy and political suicide. At Genoa there were all the forces of order, the army, the secret services of the eight most powerful – both economically and militarily – nations on the planet. Our movement can't measure up with that type of military power. We would be crushed within three months . . . Two, three years ago we thought at length about how to act in a conflict without it becoming destructive. Our technique was different: we stated publicly what we wanted to do, letting it be known that if the police attacked us, we would defend ourselves only with shields and padding. It was our rule because it was essential that we create conflict and consensus about the objectives that we set up for ourselves. In Genoa we expected that more or less the same thing as

usual would happen. They deceived us ... The police forces used firearms, even though they had assured us that they would not. The right to demonstrate that [Italian Foreign Minister Renato] Ruggiero agreed was an inalienable right was run over under the wheels of the police armoured cars.[57]

The right-wing government of Silvio Berlusconi had dramatically altered the rules of the game. In doing so it drew attention to a truth long stressed by classical Marxism – that the state, as concentrated and organized violence, acts as the last line of defence of capitalist property relations. After Genoa, an intense debate developed within the anti-capitalist movement over whether or not it should abandon mass protests altogether for fear of the violence they were attracting, both from the police and from the Black Bloc (which many believed had been infiltrated by agents provocateurs).[58] But the deeper difficulty posed by Genoa concerned how the movement could confront the centralized power of the capitalist state without reproducing the hierarchical and authoritarian structures it was seeking to challenge. Celebrations of fragmentation and dispersal are of no help whatsoever in addressing this problem.

(3) *Imperialism and war*. If Genoa revealed the domestic face of state violence, the war in Afghanistan exposed its external face. 11 September gave pause to even the most militant reformist leaders. In the debate after Genoa on 20–1 July 2001, Bello was one of those who argued that the movement should not abandon the streets.[59] Nevertheless, he regarded Genoa as a 'triumph' that was 'almost spoiled' by the violence of the Black Bloc. 9–11 had thrown the movement onto the defensive, while the successful WTO meeting at Doha in November 2001 showed that 'the other side has learned': the 'war on terrorism' had permitted the global establishment to forge a united front and force their opponents onto the defensive. The movement was left 'struggling to regain the initiative'.[60]

This analysis was not so much mistaken – 11 September had thrown North American activists into disarray, and Doha was undoubtedly a victory for the proponents of neo-liberal globalization – as one-sided. It left out of account the way in which, against the background of the radicalization that followed Genoa, opposition to the war in Afghanistan and solidarity with the Palestinian people led to an extension of the movement in Europe, and its development into a movement against imperialism and war, as well as against global capitalism. Implicit in Bello's analysis (which was shared by Susan George and other members of the ATTAC leadership) was a tendency to regard opposition to corporate globalization as a distinct cause from campaigning against militarism and war. But, as we saw in the previous chapter, these issues are not so easily separated. In his more analytical work Bello has shown a strong awareness of the connections between imperialism and capitalist globalization; it is critical to the future of the anti-capitalist movement that this awareness informs its practice as well.[61] Perhaps the caution displayed by the ATTAC leadership, who did not, at least immediately, translate their formal opposition to the 'war on terrorism' into their campaigning activity, reflected a more traditional reformist propensity to treat politics and economics as separate practices rather than aspects of an integrated totality.[62]

(4) *Class and power*. The Bush administration's war-drive brings into even sharper focus the problem posed by the Genoa protests. The movement's developing challenge to neo-liberalism and war is bringing it into conflict with the global structures of economic and military power. Whatever alternative it favours to these structures, how can it confront the vast capabilities of coercion and destruction that they embody? The autonomists' response amounts essentially to an evasion of this problem. Indeed, Toni Negri explicitly thematizes his political strategy through the metaphors of desertion and exodus:

when we speak of 'desertion', we aren't appealing to a negative slogan. It was negative when desertion was expressed
simply in terms of strikes: when it was capital and it alone
that could dispose of all the means of production, then the
strike, desertion, could only be negative. Today, if one
deserts, if one opposes the relations of power or the nexus
of capital, the relations of power or the nexus of knowledge, the relations of power or the nexus of language, one
does it in a powerful [*puissante*] way, in producing at the
very moment when one refuses. With this production – not
only of subjectivity but also of material goods, desertion
becomes a formidable keystone of the struggle. We should
explore the hackers' world to find a model of this kind. It
is a matter of models or the construction of networks that
operate at the very moment of 'subtraction', that's to say
the very moment when one rejects or eludes the capitalist
organization of production, the capitalist production of
power.[63]

This is hardly the most clearly stated of strategies, but
it seems to converge with the localist idea of creating networks of alternative production and distribution outside
the dominant set of economic relations. The obvious
problem with this strategy of desertion is that it does
nothing to address the enormous concentration of productive resources in the hands of the capitalist classes and
the states allied to them. It is, after all, this highly unequal
distribution that the anti-capitalist movement is trying to
challenge because it is the source of so much injustice and
suffering in the world today. Moreover, this distribution
means that any attempt to develop alternative economic
relationships takes place on highly unfavourable terms and
is subject to the permanent danger of incorporation. It is
to Colin Hines's credit that he explicitly addresses this
problem when advocating localization as an alternative to
neo-liberal globalization:

> TNCs . . . will use all their financial and political might to
> counter this form of localization, since it significantly
> undermines their power base. However, should citizens'

movements persuade powerful groupings of governments in Europe and/or North America to use their political power to make the necessary changes in trade rules, they would find their politician's power to regulate these entities is often underestimated. The power centres of international business are still nationally embedded, even though many have subsidiaries throughout the world. Their controlling operations are therefore not beyond the reach of national and economic bloc regulation.[64]

Hines's strategy is essentially the same as that of the more moderate ATTAC leaders. But it takes us back to the problem posed earlier: from where would the power come to tear nation-states away from their current commitment to the policies of the Washington Consensus? This question cannot be answered without a consideration of the social structure of contemporary capitalism. The movement against corporate globalization is more than anything else a response to the persistence and indeed growth of structural inequalities at both global and national levels. In the past, these inequalities were conceptualized through various theories of class. But the severe defeats suffered by the organized working class in the North in the past quarter-century have encouraged the belief that contemporary societies – at least in the advanced capitalist world – cannot be understood using class concepts. Postmodernism was probably the most influential attempt to theorize this belief, by presenting a fragmented world in which mobile individuals form plural and shifting identities unanchored in the relations of production.[65] Hardt's and Negri's concept of the multitude is a kind of compromise formation, an attempt to accommodate this thematic of plurality and multiplicity within a framework that acknowledges that different subjectivities can act in common.

The belief that class was finished was always false, and it is time that it was finally interred. On the one hand, it is commonly acknowledged that wealth and power are increasingly concentrated at the top of the global socio-political hierarchy. On the other hand, the processes of proletarianization that Marx and Engels portrayed in the *Communist Manifesto* continue on a world scale. Indeed, to the extent that the globalization of capital has taken place, the effect has been to increase the numbers of wage-labourers worldwide. A 1995 World Bank study estimated that, out of a total global non-domestic labour force of 2,474 million, 880 million people were employed, compared to 1,000 million people working for their own account on the land, and 480 million people working for their own account in industry and services.[66] These figures under-estimate the number of those dependent on wage-labour, since the massive inflows from the countryside into Third World cities over the past generation reflect the fact that many peasants and many economic actors classified as belonging to the informal sector cannot survive without intermittent or part-time wage employment.

What is the significance of these statistics? For Marx, the importance of class lay in its relationship to *power*. Capital was, he insisted, not a self-subsistent entity, but a relation: the profits of the capitalists were derived from the exploitation of wage-labour. This gave workers, when they organized collectively, the capacity to hit the capitalist class hard if they withdrew their labour-power and there-fore cut off the flow of surplus-value; but, Marx argued, workers also had both the collective capacity and the inter-est required to overthrow capitalist relations of production and replace them with a new form of society in which neither class nor exploitation would exist.[67] It is this asserted connection between class and power that is prob-ably the main reason why even many people from a tra-ditional left-wing background no longer attach much significance to class analysis: they discount the working class as an agent of social transformation.[68]

As I have already suggested, this scepticism is largely a response to the relative marginalization of organized labour in the advanced economies since the late 1970s. But this undeniable reality needs to be set in its context. The defeats suffered, particularly by certain vanguard groups of industrial workers – for example, Fiat car-workers in 1979–80 and the British miners in 1984–5 – was part of a large-scale process of capital restructuring in response to the world economy's entry into an era of crises in the early 1970s. This involved the radical 'down-sizing' of certain traditional manufacturing and extractive industries in the North and a shift of some labour-intensive production to the more advanced areas of the South. But even where the manufacturing workforce has fallen in absolute terms (by no means a universal trend in the advanced economies), increases in productivity mean that, per head, industrial workers account for a far larger output of goods than they did a generation ago. While manufacturing has generally declined as a share of national income, this sector continues to play a strategic economic role, particularly with respect to export performance and profitability. Meanwhile, the mass of workers in private and public services find themselves subject to the same pressures to produce efficiently experienced by industrial workers. Governments' and employers' demands for greater labour flexibility have certainly created a general climate of insecurity, but they have not reduced the bulk of the workforce to temporary labourers: 92 per cent of the employed in Britain held permanent job contracts in 2000, compared to 88 per cent in 1992.[69] Similarly, foreign direct investment has, as we have already seen, been concentrated in the more advanced portions of the Third World: the multinationals are attracted to areas where they can find high-quality infrastructure and a stable and well-educated workforce. These latter qualities, once again, give the workers concerned a strategic economic position that, as the development of Third World labour movements has shown, they have not been slow to exploit.[70]

This admittedly summary overview of the social changes of the past quarter-century suggests that the problem with the working class is not a structural one – the working class hasn't simply disappeared from the relations of production. It is rather one of collectivity – that is, of the extent to which the heterogeneous categories of wage-labourers can succeed in forging themselves into a collective actor.[71] Battered, fragmented, reduced in numbers, the organized working class in the advanced economies has retreated dramatically from the self-confident, centre-stage role that it played during the great socio-political upheavals of the late 1960s and early 1970s. As some trade-union leaders have begun to recognize, the emergence of the anti-capitalist movement provides an opportunity for organized labour to go onto the offensive, as part of a larger coalition against neo-liberalism. At the same time, large-scale trade-union involvement gives anti-capitalist mobilizations a social weight that they would otherwise lack. The presence of organized labour was an important feature of the most significant protests to date – Seattle (November 1999), Quebec City (April 2001), Genoa (July 2001), Barcelona (March 2002), Seville (June 2002).

Acknowledging the strategic role of the organized working class need in no way threaten the anti-capitalist movement's rightly prized diversity. It does not imply an acceptance of the moral priority of workers' claims over those of other groups oppressed by global capitalism. Marx in his mature economic writings did not claim that the working class *suffered* more than anyone else: he knew perfectly well that most industrial workers were, on the whole, materially better off than most peasants (in our day as well as his the largest group of direct producers on the planet). The claim of justice is for everyone to have equal access to the resources they need in order to live the life they have reason to value: this is a claim based on need, not on productive contribution.[72] The significance of the working class derives from the power they have to realize what justice demands: because their exploitation is central to the functioning of capitalism, they have the collective capacity to disrupt, paralyse, and reorganize production, and therefore to redirect economic life towards a different set of priorities. For workers actually to begin to play this role will require a drastic change in the political culture of organized labour. This would mean the abandonment of what Gramsci called the 'economic-corporate' approach that focuses exclusively on immediate improvements in workers' material condition and of the pursuit of 'social partnership' with capital to which trade-union leaders are, on the whole, strongly committed, to the detriment of their members' interests. More positively, workers would need to develop a sense of themselves as part of a much wider global community of the oppressed that embraces, in the South, vast numbers of semi-proletarianized city-dwellers, peasants, and landless labourers. Not the least significant consequence of labour involvement in anti-capitalist mobilizations in First and Third Worlds alike is that it can help to cultivate this sense, movingly expressed by UPS worker Doug Sabin during the Seattle protests: 'I used to think those kids talking about the environment were just wingnuts. Now I think they're part of the big "Us" that is going to have to change the world.'[73]

Adjustments would be necessary on the anti-capitalists' side as well. Kim Moody has written perceptively about 'the relative immobility of the working class', noting: 'The very position in production and accumulation that gives this class the power to shut down society, roots it geographically. Its massive numbers and limited income prevent it from quickly moving great distances.' Moody contrasts this with 'the highly mobile, disproportionately youthful core of the global justice movement', whose impact derives from 'the mobility of its activists, across the globe and in the streets, and its tactical audacity'.[74] This contrast is not necessarily disabling. Tony Blair denounced the anti-capitalist movement as an 'anarchists' travelling circus'. In fact, it is the global elite of summiteers who can more accurately be described as a travelling circus. The greatest anti-capitalist mobilizations have reflected a kind of dialectic of the local and global, in which networks of activists do indeed move on a continental or even broader basis, but in which the bulk of the demonstrators come from the local working class. The labour movement of the Northwestern United States played a decisive role in the Seattle protests; the bulk of the protesters at Quebec City were French Canadian labour unionists, at Genoa, Italian workers and youth, at Barcelona young people and trade unionists from the city and from the rest of Catalonia. Similarly, the second World Social Forum at Porto Alegre in February 2002 attracted support primarily from youth, workers, and rural people from the city and the surrounding state of Rio Grande do Sul. At such moments the old Green slogan 'Think globally, act locally' acquires a real meaning.

The political style of some anti-capitalists can be a bigger obstacle to the involvement of trade unionists. The method of organizing through affinity groups and consensus-based decision-making is designed to be inclusive, but it can have the opposite effects. Decisions based on unanimity can reflect real efforts to reach agreement, but they can also encourage an avoidance of discussion and decision-making through behind-the-scenes bargaining between powerful actors who are, in effect, democratically unaccountable. The result can be a plethora of separately organized and differently motivated protests that can diffuse energies and create confusion. Often implicit in this style of organizing is a view of protest as a form of self-realization rather than a political action intended to achieve definite consequences. The expressive aspects of the great anti-capitalist protests are seductive indeed, but they can also lead to displays of self-regarding and occasionally dangerous forms of individualism. The equation of democracy with individual autonomy by some anti-capitalists seems closer to liberalism than to any alternative based on solidarity. When combined with the active hostility to organized labour displayed at times by autonomists, the effect of these modes of behaviour can be to make ordinary working people feel unwelcome. Democracy based on the majority principle has its own weaknesses (above all, the power of big battalions to overrule dissent) but when it works well it encourages discussion – since the weight of the argument can genuinely influence the result – and leads those involved to take responsibility for the decisions which they have helped make. These problems have so far been relatively minor – the size, youth, and energy of the protests are a far greater attractive force than the repulsion caused by the self-regarding and elitist behaviour of some activists, but the development of the movement will require it to address much more seriously and reflectively than it has so far done the nature of its own democracy.

These considerations are important from a strategic point, not just because of whatever bearing they might have on the ethical principles for which the movement stands. The main social forces involved in the December 2001 rising against neo-liberalism in Argentina were the unemployed and what is loosely called the 'middle class' (in the large, better-off white-collar workers). The neighbourhood popular assemblies thrown up as the main form through which the rising and the mass movement were organized have been widely praised as the beginnings of a new kind of direct democracy.[75] They are, however, not representative bodies, but gatherings of activists. The organized working class in Argentina continues to be dominated by the Peronist-led union federations that, because of their chiefs' nationalist commitment to partnership with establishment politicians like President Eduardo Duhalde (himself a Peronist), who was brought to office by the rising, were marginal to the mass movement. This state of fragmentation has, as we saw above, been positively welcomed by autonomists who see it as 'the condition for the affirmation of a social multiplicity' – for the advent of the multitude. It is, however, more likely to lead to a situation in which popular assemblies, lacking the social power to achieve a fundamental transformation, dwindle in size and become isolated, allowing the neo-liberal and populist right, and perhaps even the military, to regain the initiative.[76] An anti-capitalist movement that disdains to win the support of the working majority will face eventual defeat.

(5) *A non-ideological left?* The existence within the movement of such diverse views on complex issues is itself a strategic problem. Vittorio Agnoletto, for example, makes this diversity a reason for seeking to develop what he calls 'a non-ideological left': 'Our movement doesn't conceive of the world as a classical painting that we just have to copy to be able to change things . . . If we were ideological we wouldn't be able to be a pluralistic movement.'[77] Behind the suspicion of 'ideology' that Agnoletto articulates here often lurk bitter memories of the dogmatism of traditional left organizations. Many older activists are veterans of the movements of the 1960s and 1970s, when they had their fill of self-proclaimed 'Marxist-Leninist' vanguards. A consequent tendency to privilege social movements relative to political organizations is reflected in the ban on the formal representation of political parties at the World Social Forum.[78]

In fact, this ban was respected more in the breach than in the observance. The presence of formally separate World Parliamentary and Municipal Forums flooded Porto Alegre II with European social-democratic politicians. It was, moreover, evident to even the most naïve outside observer that at times the WSF was being used by the Brazilian Workers Party (which governed Porto Alegre and Rio Grande do Sul) for electoral purposes. But much more important than the exploitation of anti-capitalist forums by elected politicians is the presence of distinct ideologico-political currents within the movement itself. The various tendencies I have described earlier in this chapter offer the opponents of neo-liberalism different analyses, strategies, and programmes. They are, in effect, political parties, whether or not they explicitly describe themselves as such. Agnoletto is right to stress the pluralism of the anti-capitalist movement, but this represents not an absence of ideology, but rather the presence of rival ideolog*ies*.

This tension between different positions is increasingly widely recognized. Michael Hardt, for example, identifies two main approaches represented at Porto Alegre II – what I have called reformist anti-capitalism, which counterposes national sovereignty to neo-liberalism, and an alternative that is 'more clearly posed against capital itself, whether state regulated or not,' and that 'opposes any national solutions and seeks instead a democratic globalization'. But, Hardt continues,

> It would be a mistake . . . to try to read the division according to the traditional model of ideological conflict between opposing sides. Political struggle in the age of network movements no longer works that way. Despite the apparent strength of those who occupied centre stage and dominated the representations of the Forum, they may ultimately prove to have lost the struggle . . . Eventually they too will be swept up in the multitude, which is capable of transforming all fixed and centralized elements into so many more nodes in its indefinitely expansive network.[79]

Despite Hardt's appeal here to the novelty of 'network movements', the idea that political disagreements will somehow spontaneously resolve themselves thanks to the logic of the struggle itself has a long pedigree. It was, for example, prevalent during the Second International (1889–1914), whether in the reformist version offered by Karl Kautsky or in the revolutionary approach championed by Rosa Luxemburg. All the different versions effectively deny to politics any specificity, and accordingly they fail to acknowledge the extent to which the success of movements depends on the effective articulation of ideologies and the organized pursuit of political strategies.[80] The very emergence of the strategic problems outlined above is evidence enough that the anti-capitalist movement is not somehow exempt from these hard-won truths. Nor is the existence of systematically different approaches to these problems anything particularly to bewail. On the contrary, it is a sign of the development of the movement. The real test will be to maintain as far as possible the broad unity of the movement – particularly in the various mobilizations and forums to which it is continually giving rise – while at the same time honestly and openly discussing the issues of analysis, strategy, and programme that divide it.[81]

Summary

- The anti-capitalist movement is far from homogeneous ideologically: it encompasses a variety of political currents;
- Bourgeois anti-capitalism accepts the neo-liberal claim that market capitalism offers the solution to the problems of humankind, but argues that it should become more responsive to the criticisms of 'civil society';
- Localist anti-capitalism seeks to develop micro-relationships among producers and consumers that promote social justice and economic self-sufficiency and thereby to allow markets properly to function;
- Reformist anti-capitalism advocates a return to the more regulated capitalism of the immediate post-war era through changes at the international level (for example, the Tobin Tax) that would restore greater economic power to the nation-state;
- Autonomist anti-capitalism sees in the decentralized network forms of organizing characteristic of the movement the strategic and ethical resources from which an alternative to capitalism will emerge;
- Socialist anti-capitalism (the position outlined at more length in the next chapter) argues that the only alternative to capitalism consistent with modernity is a democratically planned economy;
- The ideological heterogeneity of the anti-capitalist movement has been expressed in a series of tensions

and debates implicit in which is the old dilemma of reform and revolution: a framework needs to be developed through which these differences can be acknowledged and discussed without compromising the unity of the movement.

– 3 –

Imagining Other Worlds

Anti-capitalist values

On the Mayday demonstrations in London in 2001 a group of cyclists carried a banner proclaiming 'GET RID OF CAPITALISM AND REPLACE IT WITH SOMETHING NICER!' The slogan was intended ironically, in order to draw attention to the vagueness of anti-capitalists' conception of their alternative to the present system. It captures the mix of motivations that have impelled the movement since its origins during the 1990s – a powerful repulsion against what exists, and the as yet relatively inarticulate hope that something better can be created. The more effort that is made to give more precise expression to that hope the clearer it will become that there are a number of competing conceptions of the alternative already present within the anti-capitalist movement. It would be amazing if this were not the case. In this chapter I argue for one such conception – namely a form of socialist democracy. But, before advancing such a conception, it would seem important to offer some criteria according to which different alternatives should be judged. In particular, to what ethical principles and conceptions are anti-capitalists committed?

In my view, any alternative to capitalism in its present form should, as far as possible, meet the requirements of (at least) justice, efficiency, democracy, and sustainability. I conceive all four as substantial values that, at least in the present context, have their own justification. Nevertheless, the conceptual context in which a particular value is articulated and defended will help to determine its content: thus, to take the case of probably the most controversial of the four values advanced here, efficiency, to treat this as a requirement *together with* justice, democracy, and sustainability is to assign it an at least partially different content from what it would have in the context of values such as, say, individual liberty, private property, and economic growth. The implication is that these conjoined values mutually constrain each other. There may therefore turn out to be tensions between them: to what extent, for example, are democracy and efficiency compatible? Finally, I say that any alternative to capitalism *in its present form* must meet these requirements in order not to beg the question of whether or not some other version of the prevailing economic system could fit the bill. Let us then consider each of these values in turn.

It seems in the first place undeniable that the movement against capitalist globalization is committed to achieving justice. Indeed, one of its alternative names is 'the global justice movement'. Let's consider briefly the content and the scope of justice. We have a much clearer understanding of what justice demands, thanks to the work over the past generation of egalitarian liberal philosophers such as John Rawls, Ronald Dworkin, and Amartya Sen. As I have argued elsewhere, they have formulated principles of justice that implicitly challenge the logic of the capitalist system (even though Rawls, Dworkin, and Sen believe that in principle their principles are consistent with – indeed may even require – some version of capitalism).[1] As is natural among philosophers, there are many differences over the correct formulation of egalitarian principles of justice. Nevertheless, there is significant convergence on the idea that individuals should be provided with the resources they require to secure equal access to the advantages they need in order to live the life they have reason to value and that liberties should be equally distributed. It is also worth drawing attention to the argument that G. A. Cohen has advanced against Rawls in particular that a just society requires more than a just social structure: it embraces also a social ethos through which individuals are motivated to behave justly towards each other. This is important because it highlights the value of solidarity, something that anti-capitalists seek to display in how they organize but also that they criticize capitalism for lacking.[2]

So justice embraces *liberty*, *equality*, and *solidarity*. It is also of literally global extension. This is a controversial matter among egalitarian liberals. Rawls, for example, formulated his principles of justice in the context of the nation-state, and has resisted the extension of his Difference Principle (according to which social and economic inequalities should be tolerated only when they benefit the worst-off) to the world as a whole.[3] This seems perverse. In the first place, one of the most powerful motivations behind an egalitarian conception of justice is the desire as far as possible to correct for the effects of what Dworkin calls 'bad brute luck' – in other words, the contingencies for which individuals bear no responsibility but that may gravely limit their life-chances.[4] The global distribution of natural resources is surely a particularly important example of these contingencies, but they are far from being simply the product of physical processes. Global warming is likely to affect people in the South particularly severely, even though the generation of greenhouse gases is heavily concentrated in the North: 25 per cent of the world's population, in the North, consumes more than 70 per cent of the world's commercial energy.[5] Second, even if one rejects the more extreme claims made about globalization, the past few decades have seen a considerable increase in the international economic interdependence that has been a significant feature of capitalism since the formation of the modern world economy. If we do live in one world, as we are constantly told, then the normative principles that govern how we live together should be operative at the global level. As Charles Beitz has argued, 'principles of distributive justice now apply in the first instance to the world as a whole, and derivatively to nation-states.'[6] Justice today can only be cosmopolitan.[7]

Efficiency is the second requirement that any alternative to capitalism in its present form must meet. It might seem like the odd man out. Certainly, it is not a value to which anti-capitalists typically appeal. And one can see why. One of the main justifications for capitalism is the superior economic efficiency that is claimed for it. Moreover, more theoretical discussions identify what is held to be a trade-off between justice and efficiency: thus it is often claimed (even by egalitarian liberals like Rawls) that an equal distribution of resources might deprive the talented of the incentive to make full use of their capacities and thus to produce as efficiently as possible. These claims are disputable: as we have already seen, Cohen argues that an egalitarian society would involve individuals having just motivations towards one another rather than using their resources to get the better of each other.[8] Moreover, when efficiency is discussed in a policy context, it tends to be more or less explicitly in terms that allow the workings of market capitalism to set the criteria of success: the costs that count are those that are reflected in the price system, and the yardstick is profits relative to these costs. The inadequacy of these measures has become more and more evident in recent decades, with the development of a growing ecological consciousness: market prices do not register the costs generated by the depletion of finite resources, or the consequences of production methods that pollute the environment.

All these objections are, in my view, entirely valid. Nevertheless, even when the demands of sustainability are taken into account, it is still legitimate to ask how well a given economic system makes use of the resources that it has available to it – that is, the resources provided by its physical environment, the capacities, natural and acquired, of the people on whose activities the system's reproduction depends, and the stock of physical assets that these activities have produced. This is an important requirement because human needs are flexible and complex, and have grown with the development of human productive capacities. It may be that sustainable development is inconsistent with the existing range of needs that humans have acquired over the past two centuries of industrial capitalism. This is an open question, to which I return below. Nevertheless, it seems to me that, other things being equal, there is good reason to prefer an economic system that is capable of sustaining a wider range of needs than the alternatives. The broader the productive capacity of the system the greater the range of choice available to people, and therefore the wider the possibilities open to individuals and communities to live the different lives that the anti-capitalist movement so strongly values. Capitalism has greatly expanded the productive capacities of humankind, but at the price of a grossly unequal distribution of the opportunities thereby created, and of the wholesale destruction of both biological and social diversity. The correct response to this experience is not a mandated retreat to a supposedly simpler form of society supported by a much lower level of productivity that allows a much narrower range of choice. The right conclusion is that we should prefer the economic system that supports the widest extension of human productive capacities – widest over time and not just at any given moment – that is consistent with the requirements of justice, democracy, and sustainability. To that extent efficiency matters.[9]

The third requirement, democracy, is, in principle, much more unproblematic. One of the main targets of the anti-capitalist movement has been the effective economic dictatorship installed by the combined operations of the multinational corporations, the financial markets, the international financial institutions, and the leading capitalist states. The remedy for such a concentration of unaccountable power would seem to be an extension of democracy. But what would that involve more concretely? Three themes emerge from the critical literature – the need to revitalize existing liberal democracy, with its passive, atomized electorates and politicians obsessed with keeping the favour of the corporate media empires and maintaining a steady flow of business donations; the demand for a democratization of the economy; and a preference for the decentralization of power. Not much thought has as yet gone into how these and other aspirations might be realized institutionally. There is, as I noted in the previous chapter, a tension in how the movement itself organizes between some activists' desire for self-expression and the need to be as inclusive as possible. One issue implicit here concerns the relationship between direct and representative democracy. These are large questions: here I concentrate on the problem of how democracy can be extended to the economy.

The final requirement, sustainability, also needs little argument to support its inclusion. From Seattle onwards the environmental destruction wreaked by global capitalism has been one of the main themes of the protests. John Bellamy Foster suggests that sustainable development implies the following conditions: '(1) the rate of utilization of *renewable* resources has to be kept down to the rate of their regeneration; (2) the rate of utilization of *non-renewable* resources cannot exceed the rate at which alternative sustainable resources are developed; and (3) pollution and habitat destruction cannot exceed the "assimilative capacity of the environment".' [10] By these criteria, of course, current development is very far from sustainable. Probably most important from the viewpoint of an alternative economic system are the steps needed to counteract global warming. Stabilizing the proportion of carbon dioxide in the atmosphere at levels that do not produce severe climate change would require drastic cuts in global emissions relative to their 1990 levels (perhaps as much as 70 per cent to reach the pre-industrial atmospheric concentrations of carbon dioxide at 280 parts per million) and the self-denying ordinance to abstain from using 75 per cent of known economically viable reserves of fossil fuels. The impact that these changes would have on productive capacities and standards of living would depend on the speed with which currently known technologies using clean and renewable sources of energy such as solar and wind power, biomass, and hydrogen fuels were put into large-scale use.[11] On the face of it, the resulting energy revolution would not in the long run require the low-consumption society demanded by some Greens (though the transitional costs in temporarily reduced living standards are harder to estimate). It is, however, difficult to see how it could take place in a capitalist framework. Not simply does the present economic system – to use the analogy provided by John McNeill (see chapter 1 above) – operate like a shark, relying on the presence of a narrow set of conditions such as stable climate, cheap water and energy, but its own processes are destroying these conditions, thereby forcing us to find a different way of living.

A note on diversity

All four values – justice, efficiency, democracy, and sustainability – were presented in the previous section as if the reasons for embracing them were universally valid. This might seem to contradict the priority that is widely attached to difference and diversity within the anti-capitalist movement. This attitude has been powerfully expressed by Marcos: 'it is necessary to build another world. A world in which there is room for many worlds. A world capable of containing all the worlds.'[12] In the background to this kind of statement is the emergence over the past generation of movements contesting different oppressions – for example, gender, race, national origin, sexual orientation, and disability. During the 1980s this consciousness of difference hardened into identity politics – that is, into the belief that possession of a particular identity had replaced all other bases of collective action – often justified through an appeal to some version of cultural relativism, according to which apparently universal principles are nothing but rationalizations of the outlook of a particular group. Politics, on this view, is reduced to a clash of rival particularisms.[13] The anti-capitalist movement has transcended identity politics by seeking to forge a new form of internationalism. But, in a rather Hegelian way, this transcendence has involved incorporating much of the content of identity politics, albeit now set in what is, in effect, a universal context. The stress on the internal diversity of the movement is more than pragmatic coalition-building: it is a positively affirmed value, and one that is reflected particularly in the condemnations of the destruction of non-European cultures by colonialism and capitalism. This is why the Zapatistas have struck such a powerful chord by championing the rights of indigenous peoples.[14]

All this is well and good, but it sometimes goes along with a degree of embarrassment about explicitly advancing universal claims: activists, for example, prefer to talk about the 'transversality' of the movement – as if by highlighting the horizontal networks in which they participate they will escape any accusation of imposing an intellectual hierarchy on others. This kind of attitude is unnecessarily defensive. To build a global movement against global capitalism of its nature is to make a universal appeal. Documents such as the 'Call of the Social Movements' issued at Porto Alegre II have no specific addressee. To talk, as Marcos does, about a '*world* in which there is room for many worlds' is to seek a universal framework in which diversity can flourish. Properly understood, an egalitarian conception of justice is not about the imposition of uniformity but about giving everyone an equal opportunity to live the life that *they* – as a specific individual, with a particular set of capacities, and life-history, and cultural background, and range of needs – have reason to value. Equality and difference are not contrasted, but interdependent values.[15] Plainly not all ways of living are consistent with egalitarian justice: it conflicts with hierarchical, authoritarian, and exploitive social relationships. But it is a confusion to think that universally valid principles necessarily command universal consent. Historical experience suggests that the demands of justice divide more than they unite. But this does not necessarily mean they are invalid. The anti-capitalist movement should not be afraid to affirm universal principles.

What's wrong with the market?

Probably the most important question to be addressed when considering alternatives to capitalism in its present form is whether or not any version of the market economy can meet the demands of justice, efficiency, democracy, and sustainability. Amartya Sen has offered a seductive case for the market:

> To be *generically* against the market would be almost as odd as being generically against all conversation between people (even though some conversations are clearly foul and cause problems for others – or even for the conversationalists themselves). The freedom to exchange words, or goods, or gifts does not need defensive justification in terms of their favourable but distant effects; they are part of the way human beings in society live and interact with each other (unless stopped by regulation or fiat). The contribution of the market mechanism to economic growth is, of course, important, but this comes only after the direct significance of the freedom to interchange – words, goods, gifts – has been acknowledged.[16]

Here Sen defends the market on the grounds of its connection with freedom: this economic form is treated as equivalent to the right to engage in voluntary economic transactions. He cites Marx's support for the North in the American Civil War as an example of how gaining the freedom to participate in the market – in this case, of black slaves to become wage-labourers – represents a liberation from forced labour.[17] Sen is throwing a little dust in our eyes here. Of course Marx regarded capitalism, where workers possess the freedom to participate in the labour market on terms of legal and political equality with their potential employers, as superior to economic systems such as slavery and feudalism in which the direct producers are physically coerced to labour for their exploiters. But he also argued that the worker's lack of access to productive resources other than her own labour-power means that she is compelled to work for the capitalist on terms that lead to her exploitation. Thus, a page after celebrating the emancipation of the American slaves, Marx writes that, as soon as the worker signed the labour-contract, 'it was discovered that he was no "free agent", that the period of time for which he is free to sell his labour-power is the period of time for which he is forced to sell it, that in fact the vampire will not let go "while there remains a single muscle, sinew or drop of blood to be exploited".'[18] Under capitalism, formal freedom coexists with real unfreedom.

More seriously, Sen claims, in effect, that 'the right to interact economically with one another' must find expression in a market economy.[19] This makes the restriction – let alone the abolition – of market mechanisms necessarily a violation of human freedom. The comparison of market exchanges to conversation has, moreover, the effect (familiar in defences of capitalism) of naturalizing the market. Human society is unimaginable without language: if markets are as basic as that, then restricting or abolishing them threatens the very functioning of human societies. But Sen here elides certain important distinctions. There are markets and markets. Karl Polanyi in his classic work *The Great Transformation* (1944) argued that in the long

run of human history economic practices have been
embedded in larger social relationships, and regulated
according to one or more of the following principles –
reciprocity, redistribution, and householding (i.e. production for one's own use). Where markets existed, they did
so in the form of local trade (fairs and market days and
the like) and long-distance trade:

> both external trade and local trade are relative to geo-
> graphical distance, the one being confined to goods which
> cannot overcome it, the other only such as can. Trade of
> this kind is rightly regarded as complementary. Local
> exchange between town and countryside, foreign trade
> between different climactic zones are based on this princi-
> ple. Such trade need not imply competition.[20]

These kinds of markets were subordinated to wider
social mechanisms. The development of a market *economy*
required both the emancipation of markets from this larger
context that restricted their operation and their radical
extension:

> A market economy is an economic system controlled,
> regulated, and directed by markets alone; order in the
> production and distribution of goods is entrusted to this
> self-regulating mechanism . . . Self-regulation implies that
> all production is for sale on the market and that all
> incomes derive from such sales. Accordingly, there are
> markets for all elements of industry, not only for goods
> (always including services) but also for labour, land, and
> money, their prices being respectively commodity prices,
> wages, rent, and interest.[21]

Land, labour, and money are, according to Polanyi,
'fictitious commodities' – they are not naturally movable
items that can be bought and sold. Concerted state intervention was required to reorganize society on the basis of
markets for land, labour, and money (Polanyi sees the
establishment of the English New Poor Law in 1834 as an

important stage in this process), and also to limit and control the potentially destructive effects of the market once transformed into a self-regulating system. The history of nineteenth-century Europe, Polanyi argues, is that of the struggle between two principles – 'economic liberalism' (whose 'three classic tenets' were 'a labour market, the gold standard, and free trade') and 'social protection', representing respectively the drive of 'the trading classes' to extend the empire of the market and the struggle of 'the working and the landed classes' to restrict it.[22]

Polanyi provides a useful historical perspective on contemporary neo-liberalism: the political efforts to reconstruct societies along the lines laid down by the Washington Consensus bear striking similarities to the efforts of Victorian liberals to make British society safe for *laissez-faire*. The distinctions he draws between different kinds of markets also allow us to reformulate the question as it is posed by Sen. What we need to establish is not whether there is something inherently wrong with human beings voluntarily exchanging goods or services, but rather whether a market economy in Polanyi's sense, which is equivalent to how Marx understood capitalism – that is, a self-regulating economic system in which as many as possible goods and services are produced to be sold on the market, and where markets for labour, land, and money exist – is consistent with a just and decent society.

It is hard to see how it could be. Consider the four requirements set out above. First, a market economy violates the requirements of justice. Individuals under capitalism do not have equal access to advantage. Not only are access to productive resources and the distribution of wealth and income grossly unequal, but individuals' life-chances are drastically affected for both the better and the worse by processes outside their control – in particular the fluctuations of the market. Think of the fortunes made, but also the lives destroyed by the financial booms and busts of the neo-liberal era. No wonder that Friedrich von Hayek, probably the most sophisticated defender of capitalism, was vehemently against appealing to any conception of social justice when appraising the relative merits of economic systems.[23] Second, the concentrations of economic power that capitalism generates gravely restrict the scope of democracy, since most citizens are deprived of any say in crucial decisions affecting their lives. Moreover, such democratic mechanisms as do exist are gravely compromised both by the corruption of political processes by corporate influence and by the severe sanctions (for example, capital flight) suffered by governments that pursue policies treated by the markets as inimical. Third, capitalism's blind flight forward, impelled by the processes of competitive accumulation that I discussed in chapter 1, has produced a mode of economic development that is demonstrably unsustainable from an ecological point of view.[24]

It is only when we introduce considerations of economic efficiency that the case for capitalism begins to look at all robust (I abstract from the question of how measures of efficiency should take into account environmental costs, in order to give capitalism a fairer run than it would otherwise receive). The collapse of the Soviet Union and most of the other Stalinist societies at the end of the 1980s has led many on the left to accept the argument – most powerfully formulated by Hayek – that a market economy is necessarily superior to any version of socialist planning in efficiently allocating resources.[25] I consider this argument more directly in the next section. For the moment I want to examine two compromise solutions that seek to retain the market but restrict its operation in order the better to meet the kind of requirements that I argue anti-capitalists in effect make. The first of these is market socialism, a hypothetical economic system that is much favoured by left-wing philosophers and economists, though their writings have had, as far as I can tell, no resonance in the anti-capitalist movement.[26] The thought is essentially to get rid of capitalist exploitation – the apparently voluntary but really unequal exchange between capitalist and worker that depends on the latter's lack of any better alternative to working for the capitalist – but retain the market. Enterprises might, for example, be run by workers' cooperatives that compete to sell their products on the market.

It should be noted first that market socialism would not remove all the sources of injustice, since individuals would continue to benefit or suffer because of factors for which they could not be held responsible – the distribution of natural talents would, for example, give some economic actors greater market power than others.[27] Of more immediate concern: could market socialism constitute a stable alternative to capitalism? It seems doubtful. In a competitive process economic actors seek to gain an advantage over their rivals – for example, by making cost-cutting innovations – that allows them to make higher than average profits. These advantages are often cumulative: the surplus-profit allows the innovator to maintain investment in continuous innovations that widen the gap that separates him from his rivals. Competition can thus increase inequalities across the economy rather than smoothing them out. At the same time, the pressure of competition can also generate inequalities within individual enterprises: the effort to raise productivity and cut costs may encourage the development of managerial hierarchies that undercut the supposedly cooperative character of production. In other words, market socialism is permanently liable to collapse back into market capitalism. To the extent that schemes for market socialism propose institutional safeguards against such tendencies they move away from anything resembling a market economy in Polanyi's sense.[28]

The second form of compromise between the market and the demands of justice, democracy, and sustainability is simply a more regulated form of capitalism than the Anglo-American *laissez-faire* model that is being promoted by the Washington Consensus. Will Hutton, for example, is an eloquent proponent of 'stakeholder capitalism', a rival model that, following the examples of post-war

Germany and Japan, regulates markets in order to maintain economic stability and social harmony.[29] As we have seen in the previous chapter, the reformist wing of the anti-capitalist movement advocates some such regulated capitalism through a combination of revived national sovereignty and greater international cooperation. Polanyi offers a longer-term perspective on this kind of proposal: he argues that the disastrous consequences of economic liberalism – made most evident by the Great Depression of the 1930s – engendered a reaction in the shape of different political movements, notably socialism and fascism, 'under which the economic system ceases to lay down the law to society and the primacy of society over that system is secured'.[30] We might consider recent experience as another turn in the same historical cycle, one in which the neo-liberal effort to dismantle the restrictions imposed on self-regulating markets between the 1930s and the 1960s has provoked the effort to build new forms of regulation in the interests of social protection.

There are at least two kinds of question that need to be addressed when considering the feasibility of alternative models of capitalism. The first concerns the compatibility of these models with the present phase of capitalist development. The global integration of financial markets that enforce the maximization of 'shareholder value' has already helped to undermine the functioning of the existing stakeholder capitalisms in continental Europe and Japan and prompted institutional reforms that bring them closer to the Anglo-Saxon model.[31] This does not mean that it is impossible for national governments to mount any challenge to the Washington Consensus, as Leo Panitch suggests when he makes the puzzling claim: 'No state, of course, could introduce capital controls (bar the American)'.[32] China's possession of capital controls allowed it to ride out the Asian financial crash of 1997–8 with comparative ease.[33] It is important not to underestimate the capacities that nation-states still possess. All the same, any national challenge would soon find itself up against an extremely powerful constellation of social forces, embedded in the existing structures of globalized finance and transnational investment and backed up by the US and the other leading capitalist states. It is hard to see how this challenge could succeed except as part of an international movement and through tremendous upheavals. After all, the relatively humane capitalism (in the West at least) of the Keynesian era was the product of two world wars, the Russian Revolution and its Stalinist aftermath, the greatest economic slump in the history of capitalism, and fascism.

But, secondly, let us suppose that an international version of reformism somehow triumphed and that the world therefore entered another era of regulated capitalism. Only a fool would deny that some versions of capitalism are more humane and fair than others. By the admittedly low standards of the past few millennia of class societies, during the 1950s and 1960s the liberal capitalisms of Western Europe and North America, for all their injustices and irrationalities, offered most of their poorer citizens a much better life than was imaginable at the start of the twentieth century – though one bought at the price of the constant danger of nuclear destruction during the Cold War.[34] But this did not prove a stable state of affairs. Confronted by the crisis of profitability that set in during the late 1960s, the leading capitalist classes began to emancipate themselves from restrictions that had seemed less onerous during the era of high profits and rapid growth after the Second World War. The result has been, in the North, the partial dismantlement of the systems of social protection that had helped to civilize capitalism and, in the South, a drive to restore a much more brutally exploitive capitalism – both processes that are very far from having reached their term. Maybe we could, through some enormous effort, manage once again to impose civilizing restrictions on capitalism. But how stable would this solution be? There seems, in other words, to be an inherent tension between the fundamental features of capitalism –

that is, its reliance on the exploitation of wage-labour and its dynamic of competitive accumulation – and the institutional structures that, as a result of both social conflicts and class compromises, impose restrictions on it. Rather than continue this oscillation between the liberation of capitalism's most destructive tendencies and their partial containment, wouldn't it be better to replace capitalism with 'something nicer'?[35]

Why we need planning

Socialist planning is generally thought to be an idea whose time has come and gone. All the same, we need it very badly. As a first approximation, by socialist planning I mean an economic system where the allocation and use of resources are determined collectively on the basis of democratic decision-making procedures central to which is the majority principle. This hypothetical economic system contrasts with pre-capitalist class societies, where allocation was also collectively regulated through the mechanisms listed by Polanyi – redistribution, reciprocity, and householding – but where these mechanisms were, on the whole, undemocratic, with key decisions being taken by aristocratic landowners, slave-owners, patriarchal heads of household, and the like. Socialist planning also contrasts with capitalism, where the allocation of resources is the unintended outcome of the competitive struggle among capitals that jointly but not collectively control the economic process. A planned socialist economy is democratic but that does not mean it would always rely on the majority principle. There are many cases in which other decision procedures are appropriate: part of the point of the concept of individual rights is to identify those areas where individuals should be able to exclude all others from participating in decisions that primarily concern them. For example, as we saw in the previous section, one of the achievements of capitalism has been to establish that individuals have the exclusive right to decide what sort of work they should undertake (even though it fails to make this right a social reality). It seems to me that a socialist economic system in general would respect and indeed extend this right.[36]

To be effective socialist planning must operate at the international level. Capitalism is a global system: there is plenty of historical experience to show that nation-states that try (in Margaret Thatcher's words) to buck the market are subject to severe sanctions – capital flight, other forms of economic isolation, political subversion, and, at the limit, armed invasion – that at best severely compromise, at worst destroy their efforts to construct alternatives to the prevailing system.[37] An alternative economic framework must therefore be constructed on an international scale. But, in any case, planning is urgently needed to address global problems. For example, one of the main issues raised by climate change is that the advantages and disadvantages produced by the current economic system's method of using resources are extremely unequally distributed. The United States, with 5 per cent of the world's population, consumes 25 per cent of its resources, while the South, whose per capita use of resources is far lower, is likely to be much more directly and adversely affected by the global warming that has been generated by this pattern of resource-consumption. Any serious attempt to reduce greenhouse gas emissions – which would mean cuts of between 50 and 70 per cent below the emission levels prevailing in 1990 (the benchmark level set by the Kyoto Protocol) – would require global mechanisms capable of negotiating and enforcing decisions designed drastically to alter the prevailing allocation and use of resources over decades. If that isn't planning, I don't know what is.

But the very idea of planning on a global scale dramatizes the major objection to a planned economy, that it is necessarily highly centralized, with damaging implications for both efficiency and democracy. The efficiency objection was most powerfully put by Hayek in what is probably the classic critique of planning. He argues that the market offers, via the fluctuations of relative prices, a highly flexible and decentralized mechanism for transferring between economic actors the information they require in order to arrive at the most efficient means for meeting their individual needs. By contrast a planned economy transfers information upwards to the centre where all decisions that matter are made. Since the information assembled at the centre is too vast, complex, and diverse to be processed, the result is hypertrophy, paralysis, and chaos.[38] One might also consider localism as expressing the aspiration, in opposition to both capitalist globalization and socialist planning, for decentralized and democratic forms of economic cooperation.

Implicit in both the neo-liberal and the localist objections is a preference for horizontal transactions among economic actors who relate to each other on a basis of rough equality, as opposed to the vertical, top-down set-up that they assert is a necessary feature of a planned economy. Sen's comparison of the market to a conversation implicitly presents it as a non-hierarchical, inter-individual relationship (or set of relationships). Two points are worth making in response. First, actually existing capitalism is very far from being a cluster of horizontal transactions – the 'network society' celebrated by its contemporary apologists.[39] Only a handful of privileged economic actors – in particular, those participating in the real networks that control the major multinational corporations and investment banks – are involved in anything remotely resembling authentically horizontal relationships. Most people are caught in vertical relations of domination and subordination. Second, it is undoubtedly true that the bureaucratic command economy created by the 'Stalin revolution' in the Soviet Union at the end of the 1920s and transplanted to the other Stalinist states after the Second World War closely resembled the supposedly omnicompetent but really incompetent planning centre portrayed by Hayek and his followers (though the neo-liberal critique is of no use in explaining why this peculiar system developed).[40] But it in no sense follows from this historical experience that a planned economy must necessarily take this form.

The hopes in a feasible alternative to capitalism lie in a planned economy based, not on the vertical impositions of the centre, but on decentralized, horizontal relationships among producers and consumers. Commenting on Alec Nove's defence of market socialism, Pat Devine writes:

> Nove's challenge must not be forgotten: 'There are horizontal links (market), there are vertical links (hierarchy). What other dimension is there?'... There is no other dimension – but vertical links do not have to be hierarchical, in any authoritarian sense, and horizontal links do not have to be market-based, in the sense of being coordinated *ex post* by the invisible hand of market forces. Both can be based on negotiated coordination.[41]

On this basis Devine develops a 'model of democratic planning ... in which planning takes the form of a political process of negotiated coordination, with decisions being made, directly or indirectly, by those who are affected by them'.[42] Broad economic parameters – covering such matters as the macro-economic division of resources between individual and collective consumption, social and economic investment, energy and transport policies, and environmental priorities – would be decided nationally by the elected representative assembly on the basis of a set of alternative plans drafted by experts.[43] But, within this framework, the bulk of economic decision-making would take place on a decentralized basis. Economic power would be vested in negotiated coordination bodies for individual production units and sectors on which would sit representatives of the workforce, consumers, suppliers, relevant government bodies, and concerned interest groups.

In the model of negotiated coordination, the relative prices of goods and services would be set at levels that

allowed production units to cover their costs and realize the surplus needed to meet the planned allocation
of output for investment, but that would also take into
account the social costs represented by the use of renewable and non-renewable natural resources. Units or sectors
that failed to realize the necessary surplus would be
permitted to continue in operation where the relevant
negotiated coordination bodies decided that it was socially
desirable for a subsidy to be applied. Thus 'the necessary
information for effective centralized and decentralized
decision-making in the social interest is generated without recourse to "market forces" . . . by a combination of
socially shaped demand- and cost-based prices, on the
one hand, and interest-based decision-making on the
other.' As a result, Devine argues, '[n]egotiated coordination bodies would allow economic decisions to be coor-
dinated consciously, yet without central administrative
command, in the light of the overall situation, yet on a
sufficiently decentralized basis to make effective use of
local knowledge.'[44]

Though worked out in detail for a national economy,
according to Devine 'the principles underlying the model
of negotiated coordination could be applied to international economic transactions' – indeed, given what I have
already argued, it is crucial that they could be. The most
obvious objection to the model is the time consumed
in the decision-making process, particularly given the
complex interests spread across an entire country or even
the globe that would have to be reconciled in particular
cases. Devine comments: 'In modern societies a large and
possibly increasing proportion of overall social time is
already spent on administration, on negotiation, on organizing and running systems,' though 'much of this activity
is . . . concerned with commercial rivalry and the management of the social conflict and consequences of alienation
that stem from exploitation, oppression, inequality and
subalternity'. He concludes that

there is no *a priori* reason to suppose that the aggregate time devoted to running a self-governing society based on negotiated coordination would be greater than the time devoted to the administration of people and things in existing society. However, aggregate time would be differently composed, differently focused and, of course, differently distributed among people.[45]

These points deserve to be made more emphatically and extended. First, a relatively small number of people – corporate executives, investment bankers, consultants of variant sorts – currently spend their highly paid working time taking meetings in which decisions are made that shape the lives of most people on the planet. Democratic planning of the kind represented by Devine's model of negotiated coordination would end this structure of domination and subordination by transferring decision-making power – and therefore time – to the mass of producers and consumers. Second, even if it were the case that this redistribution did lead to major economic decisions taking longer, would this be such a terrible thing? One of the main characteristics of the capitalist perpetual motion machine is the speed with which it drives blindly towards financial crashes, economic crises, and, in the longer term, environmental catastrophe. We could do with slowing down a bit. It is impossible to say whether the introduction of something like negotiated coordination would lead to a fall in the long-term growth rate without considering the saving that could be made under such a model of the output wasted by economic instability and military competition and the benefits that would flow from the introduction of methods of economic calculation that took proper account of environmental costs. Third, Devine's model could be strengthened to ensure proper scope for innovation: resources could be set aside at the local, regional, national, and international level for which competing teams could bid to gain support for their favoured schemes. Investment banks, venture capitalists, and equity markets currently perform this role, but on the basis of the expected profits such proposals would generate rather than the social benefits they could bring.

Assessing these potential benefits would inevitably be a contested process. Individuals have different desires, projects, and ideals that are not always easily reconcilable, and therefore approach issues with attitudes coloured by their particular interests. Devine writes: 'The social principle is never transparently evident. Self-activating equal subjects need to engage together at every level of decision-making in order to decide themselves what in detail constitutes the social interest in every situation.'[46] An essential condition for these processes to be relatively harmonious, ending in agreement or at least in the minority's reasonably ungrudging acceptance of the majority decision, is that citizens enjoy equality of access to the resources they require in order to live the lives they have reason to value. This would allow them to participate in perhaps hotly contested decisions on the basis of broad economic security, but also with a sense of being engaged in a shared enterprise in which the distribution of benefits and burdens was fairly allocated. Equality, in other words, is not simply a normative principle that a socialist society should seek to realize but a functional requirement of such a society.

How equal access to advantage could begin to be realized is something to which I return in the next section. For the moment, I wish to stress an important implication of any model of decentralized planning such as Devine's. Its functioning would not simply both depend on and help to secure an egalitarian society: it would also require the social ownership of at least the most important impersonal productive resources. François Chesnais, Claude Serfati, and Charles-André Udry have criticized the anti-capitalist movement for avoiding the issue of which forms of property are compatible with its objectives:

> The exercise of a social, collective, 'citizen' mastery of the conditions of commercial exchanges among peoples, as of

the organization of work and the satisfaction of urgent social needs, supposes that we stop considering the question of the forms of property of the means of production, communication, and exchange as a taboo question, a question which the crisis and collapse of state property that was collectivized in a bureaucratic or Stalinist fashion, had settled once and for all.[47]

As Chesnais, Serfati, and Udry point out, leading business interests show a vivid sense of the importance of property-forms when they lobby international financial institutions for the protection of property rights, demand that governments privatize public services, and promote the broader process of securitization that transforms everything possible into vendible financial assets. The logic of capitalist globalization is that of commodification, its outcome is to disaggregate the world into parcels of exclusive private property. It is hard to see how this logic can be replaced by one based on the democratic determination of shared needs without extensive social ownership of impersonal productive resources. How could decisions be taken democratically about the allocation of resources if these resources were, in the main, privately owned? The essence of private property is that it confers on the owner the right to exclude others from decisions over the use of the items she owns. A democratically planned economy would have to be based on social ownership.

Two qualifications are necessary to this argument. First, it does not require that *all* productive resources are socially owned. As has already been noted, people should be free to choose their occupation. Moreover, the scope for small enterprise would have to be democratically negotiated: the sorry experience of forced collectivizations in the twentieth century suggests that land reform should often, at least in the first instance, take the form of an extension of peasant proprietorship.[48] Second, to advocate social ownership is not to defend the bureaucratic forms of state property that were generally seen in the twentieth century as the alternative to market capitalism. Chesnais, Serfati, and Udry rightly insist: '*Social ownership is an imposture, if it is not accompanied by forms of management and truly collective and democratic control.*'[49] But then central to the model of socialist planning outlined here is a radical extension of democracy in two respects: first, economic processes would now be subjected to collective decision-making, and, second, decision-making would itself be decentralized on the basis of negotiated coordination. These changes would give meaning to the slogan of 'participatory democracy' and thereby counteract the tendency towards citizens' withdrawal from politics that is such a disturbing feature of contemporary liberal democracies.[50]

Naturally this brief outline only sketches out some of the main features of a planned socialist economy and leaves many important questions unanswered. It nevertheless seems superior to the main alternative conceptions current in the anti-capitalist movement, localization and fair trade. As a micro-reform, fair trade may benefit particular groups of Third World producers – though, where primary commodities are over-produced, one farmer's success will be another's loss. Moreover, as Naomi Klein has noted, 'the challenges of a global labour market are too vast to be defined – or limited – by our interests as consumers'.[51] At my local supermarket I can now buy Fair Trade bananas and coffee, but as an individual consumer I lack the time or resources to ensure that these commodities have really been produced under the conditions laid down by the Fair Trade movement. Addressing the problems of global injustice requires collective, not individual solutions. Extended to the international scale, localist strategies can go one of two ways. One, defended by Colin Hines, for example, is to maximize national self-sufficiency and minimize long-distance trade.[52] This represents a break with more than capitalism since, as we have seen, long-distance trade has been practised by human societies for thousands of years. It is, moreover, in effect to renounce the productive capacities that we now possess thanks to the development of a world economy. But why should international economic connections be treated as a priori undesirable? It is undoubtedly an obscenity that farms in Zimbabwe produce flowers and mange-touts for export when millions of local people go hungry. But, equally, why should rural producers return to the vulnerability to vicissitudes of weather and disease that was their unavoidable fate in premodern times? Our existing productive capacities (not to speak of those we could develop on their basis) allow us the means to address the gross inequalities that render the contemporary world such a wretched place. We should not lightly throw them away.

Alternatively, fair trade, when it is treated as the framework of a new international system, may approximate to the model of negotiated coordination that I have been discussing in this section. Michael Barratt Brown, for example, imagines community councils forming 'horizontal linkages' for the exchange of goods and services. 'Contracts and prices would then be the subject of negotiation on quality and service between representatives of the workers, the groups of households and the elected local authority at district level.' National and international representative bodies would set 'general parameters of resource allocation', but 'the communities and districts form the real building blocks of decentralized power', acting as the nodes of overlapping networks of fair trade. Barratt Brown insists that '[t]he networks could not be said to be effective, competing traders if they could not set their own prices and make their own investments.'[53] But the picture he paints is one in which prices would reflect a process of negotiation among collective actors where the criteria of success would be, as far as possible, meeting the needs of the participants rather than maximizing profitability. Such an economic system is clearly radically different from the self-regulating market economy critically analysed by Marx and Polanyi. Once market exchanges have been systematically subordinated to democratic decision-making processes driven by the claims of need, then, even if prices and money continue to play a role as convenient accounting devices, there is little sense in calling the resulting system a market economy. The evils of capitalism can only be overcome, not by rescuing the market, but by replacing it.

A transitional programme

Socialist planning, conceived along something like the lines sketched out by Pat Devine in his model of negotiated coordination, is both a feasible and a desirable alternative to capitalism. But we are a long way from it. Indeed, the neo-liberal policies of the Washington Consensus are driving us in the opposite direction, towards a world where everything becomes fungible, a commodity to be bought and sold for profit. A movement that is seeking to reverse this process must therefore organize mass struggles to demand measures that would both offer immediate remedies and begin to introduce a different social logic. The following suggestions are intended more in the spirit of discussion than as a finished programme:

- *Immediate cancellation of Third World debt*: One of the most visible signs of the injustice that currently reigns is the fact that some of the poorest countries in the world are forced to spend a high proportion of their foreign earnings on debt repayments to some of the richest institutions in the world, the banks and governments of the North. The G7 'debt relief' scheme promoted in particular by the British Chancellor of the Exchequer Gordon Brown is a cruel deception, since it makes relief conditional on the governments concerned adopting 'reforms' that further the neo-liberal agenda. The demand for the immediate and unconditional cancellation of Third World debt helped to bring the anti-capitalist movement into being and it continues to be an urgent priority.

- *Introduction of the Tobin Tax on international currency transactions*: Debt cancellation would only be a first step in addressing the plight of much of the South: it would not generate new resources to promote development of the right kind. One of the attractions of the Tobin Tax is that it could fund a significant degree of redistribution from North to South. Some form of international institution would be necessary to organize this, since otherwise the bulk of the revenues would remain in the advanced economies where most currency transactions take place. Introducing the tax would also begin to restore a degree of political control on financial markets. The effects should not, however, be exaggerated. Bruno Jetin and Suzanne de Brunhoff note: 'There are two clear limitations to the Tobin tax: first, it does not stop major speculative attacks on a given currency. And second, it does not solve the problems caused by the disappearance of the previous international monetary system, and by the fact that it has not been replaced.'[54] It is because of these limitations that the much more ambitious systemic transformation outlined in the previous section is necessary. Nevertheless, the Tobin Tax is a worthwhile reform, both as a potential mechanism for global redistribution and for its role in denaturalizing the market and demonstrating that economic processes can be politically governed.
- *Restoration of capital controls*: International law still allows states to impose capital controls under the 1944 Bretton Woods agreement that set up the IMF and the World Bank, but these institutions now do everything possible to press governments to follow the example of the advanced economies since the late 1970s and renounce capital controls. Reintroducing them would allow governments to exert some control over the

inflow and outflow of capital – the driving force behind the 'emerging market' financial crashes of the past decade or so. Their efficacy would only be limited: Britain, for example, suffered a series of severe currency crises during the post-war era despite the state's powers to regulate capital movements (which were renounced by the Thatcher government in 1979). But, like the Tobin Tax, capital controls would begin to establish some degree of political control of financial markets, in this case at the national level.

- *Introduction of universal basic income*: The basis of capital's power lies, however, in its control of production, not in the financial markets. One of the attractions of the idea that every citizen be granted as of right a basic income set, say, at a level that would allow them to meet their socially recognized subsistence needs is that it could help to emancipate workers from the dictatorship of capital. Such a basic income would radically alter the bargaining power between labour and capital, since potential workers would now be in a position, if they chose, to pursue alternatives to paid employment. Moreover, because all citizens would receive the same basic income (perhaps with adjustments for economic handicaps such as age, disability, and dependent children), its introduction would be an important step towards establishing equality of access to advantage.

- *Reduction of the working week*: The slow growth of the past quarter-century has led to a state of affairs in which, through much even of the advanced capitalist world, overwork and enforced idleness coexist. For those on both terms of this relationship, this is a destructive and wasteful situation. A significant reduction in the working week – say, to thirty hours a week in the advanced economies – would lead to a fairer distribution of work by increasing the rate of employment. Supporting this demand does not mean accepting what orthodox economists call 'the lump of labour fallacy', according to which there is only a limited amount of work to go round. Reducing the working week need not reduce productivity and may be accompanied by higher output thanks to the consequent fall in the rate of unemployment. Wage-earners could use the shorter working week not merely to engage in leisure activities but also to participate in the decision-making processes that a collectively managed economy would require.

- *Defence of public services and renationalization of privatized industries*: The neo-liberal drive to privatize public services cannot be justified by some neutral standard of efficiency – by 'what works', as Tony Blair never tires of claiming. Privatization works to the benefit of a coalition of politicians, investment bankers, and corporate executives who stand to profit both from the process through which public assets are floated on the market and from the provision of privatized services with the aim of maximizing 'shareholder value'.[55] The catastrophe undergone by the British railway system since its privatization under the Tories amply illustrates the conflict between private profit and the social interest. Even the Blair government, dogmatically wedded as it is to the Washington Consensus, has been forced to make concessions to the overwhelming public support for the renationalization of the railways by forcing Railtrack (which owns the rail infrastructure) into receivership. The presumption should be that privatized industries be returned to public ownership. Meanwhile, neo-liberal 'reforms' of public services, which are typically intended to introduce mechanisms mimicking market forces into the realm of social provision, usually through processes of bureaucratic centralization reminiscent of a Stalinist command economy, should be resisted. The defence of the existing public sector is in no sense incompatible with the exploration of alternative forms of democratic social ownership.[56]

- *Progressive taxation to finance public services and redistribute wealth and income*: One feature of the neo-liberal era has been a shift from direct to indirect taxation, and a general reduction in the tax burden on corporations and the wealthy. The effect is to increase the share of taxation paid by the poor at the same time as (because of spending cuts and market 'reforms') they benefit less from the public services that they help to finance. Higher rates of direct taxation – above all progressive income tax – would help to provide public services with the resources of which they have been starved by neo-liberal policies. Moreover, by requiring the better off to contribute a substantially larger share of their income and wealth, this shift in the tax burden would promote greater economic and social equality.

- *Abolition of immigration controls and extension of citizenship rights*: One of the most flagrant contradictions of neo-liberalism is that it promotes the global mobility of capital while restricting that of labour. Labour is significantly less mobile internationally than it was during the first era of capitalist globalization a century ago.[57] In consequence, we are confronted with the repellent sight of the rich countries erecting ever higher barriers against the wretched of the earth, who are driven to seek refuge in the North because of miseries of injustice, poverty, and war whose ultimate cause is the present economic system. The persecution of asylum-seekers and their confinement in privatized detention centres in defiance of international law is becoming a moral scandal in many OECD countries, with Australia leading the way while others eagerly follow. If we live in a globalized world, as the clichés have it, then freedom of movement about it should be a universal right, rather than relatively unrestricted mobility being one of the privileges of the citizens of the rich countries. It follows also that citizenship should cease to flow from descent, and become a right consequent on a certain period of residence. Such a move would acknowledge the reality of international mobility (despite states' efforts to restrict it) by enabling people to participate in the political process where they have chosen to live and work. It would also end the flagrant injustice whereby in countries such as Germany large immigrant populations are disenfranchised despite long residence or birth there.[58]

- *A programme to forestall environmental catastrophe*: The most serious long-term threat to both humankind and the planet comes from the processes of environmental destruction unleashed by the unrestrained accumulation of capital. The United Nations *Global Environment Outlook-3*, published in May 2002, outlines four scenarios for the next generation. The two that most closely correspond to current global arrangements – 'Market First' and 'Security First' – imply the acceleration during the period 2002–32 of the processes of destruction already under way.[59] Preventing this grim future from becoming actual will require a systematic reversal of priorities. This demands a programme in its own right embracing, among many other measures, the international adoption of enforceable targets for drastic reductions in greenhouse emissions, large-scale public investment in the generation and distribution of renewable energy and in the development of cheap public transport, and the much longer-term restructuring of our increasingly urbanized societies in order to transform current patterns of settlement and distribution based on growing dependence on the internal combustion engine.

- *Dissolution of the military-industrial complex*: The fall in global military expenditure after the end of the Cold War proved to be a blip. In 1999 arms spending rose for the first time since 1988. George W. Bush's war drive is likely to reinforce this trend: the administration's January 2002 budget proposed to increase defence spending by $120 billion in the following five years.[60] Claude Serfati itemizes some of the main features of the broader process of 'armed globalization' of which these statistics are a symptom: 'the transformation of the conditions of arms production and the central role that finance capital plays there, the increasing integration of civil and military technologies, the multiplication of types of weapon of mass destruction (chemical and bacteriological), but also their easier proliferation. The militarization of the planet at the dawn of the twenty-first century presents redoubtable dangers.'[61] These dangers are by no means confined to the activities of the advanced capitalist states. One consequence of the war in Afghanistan was to stoke up tensions between South Asia's two nuclear powers, India and Pakistan. But the *Financial Times* noted: 'While the international community calls for restraint on the Indo–Pakistan border, governments led by the UK and the US are jockeying as never before for a bigger slice of India's growing arms budget.' Among the visitors to New Delhi attracted by the $5 billion India spends annually on military hardware were the British Foreign Secretary, Jack Straw, and the US Chairman of the Joint Chiefs of Staff, General Richard Myers.[62] Military expenditures generated by geopolitical competition at the global and regional level threaten appalling destruction; it also represents a huge diversion of resources from socially worthwhile uses. Responding to this set of problems would once again require a programme in its own right embracing the dissolution of NATO, universal nuclear disarmament, drastic cuts in arms budgets, the more general demilitarization of the globe, and public support for the conversion of military industries to civilian purposes.

• *Defence of civil liberties*: Even before 11 September, some Western governments (notably the British) had introduced legislation that could be used to prosecute peaceful protesters as terrorists. The 'war on terrorism' has legitimized a much more extensive assault on civil liberties, extending in the US to the arbitrary detention and deportation of aliens without recourse to the courts and their liability to prosecution for terrorism by military commissions allowed by presidential decree to sentence prisoners to death by much lower standards than those prevailing in civilian courts. The anticapitalist movement must therefore seek to defend civil liberties, for its own sake, and also because it has taken up the challenge of combating the erosion of citizenship rights that has become such a marked feature of this era of 'democratic governance'.

This list of demands is merely indicative. Others could come up with more extensive and imaginative programmes, and the one outlined here no doubt reflects to a significant extent the preoccupations of intellectuals and activists in the North. But then it would be both silly and pretentious to sit in London and attempt to come up with, say, a programme that would address the plight of the landless in Brazil. There are two features of this programme that are of more general relevance. First, the demands listed above are generally placed on states acting either singly or in concert. This reflects the fact that, whatever the effects of globalization, states are still the most effective mechanisms in the world as currently constituted for mobilizing resources to achieve collectively agreed goals. To recognize this is not to renege on anything that I have said earlier about the limitations of any political strategy that identifies the nation-state as the main counter-weight to global capitalism. States are part of the capitalist system, not a countervailing power to it. But states, because they are at least partially dependent on securing the consent of their subjects, are vulnerable to political pressure from below. Mass movements can therefore extract reforms from them. It is, however, crucial to understand that any such concessions will be won, not through negotiations with ostensibly sympathetic governments, but through mass struggles. The reforms outlined above go against the logic of capital. They can only be won by a movement that maintains its political independence and that has the power, thanks to the central role played within it by the organized working class, to wrest concessions from the system. The anti-capitalist movement should not be afraid of putting demands on states, but it should maintain its independence of them.

Easier said than done, some might say: engaging with states to achieve reforms might easily lead to the movement's incorporation. This is a real enough danger. The ambiguity of reform*ism* as a political strategy is that it represents both a challenge to the system and a means of containing that challenge. There is no easy way round this problem. To refuse to seek any partial improvement for fear of contamination by the status quo has always been one of the prime marks of the political sectarian and dogmatist. But here a second feature of the programme outlined above is worth noting. As I have already indicated, all the demands listed are directly at odds with the neoliberal elite consensus. Even the most moderate – say, a shift from indirect to direct taxation – would seem, from the standpoint of this consensus, to be utterly unrealistic. For all that, these demands aren't just a wish list plucked from the air. They represent responses to contemporary realities, and have all been raised by existing movements. At the same time, the tendency of these demands is to undermine the logic of capital. For example, to introduce universal direct income at a relatively generous level would severely compromise the present workings of the labour market, and thereby remove one of the essential conditions of capitalist exploitation. In other words, while not necessarily formulated for explicitly anti-capitalist reasons, these demands have an implicitly anti-capitalist dynamic. They are what Trotsky called transitional demands, reforms that emerge from the realities of existing struggles but whose implementation in the current context would challenge capitalist economic relations.[63]

A movement therefore that succeeded in achieving even the partial implementation of such a programme by, let us say, a particular nation-state would be faced with a dilemma. In all probability, even these limited successes would have sufficiently disrupted the functioning of capitalism in the country in question to cause significant economic damage through such mechanisms as capital flight, a run on the currency, and a sharp rise in the inflation rate. The movement could react by retreating and perhaps cooperating in the restoration of 'confidence' at the price, over time, of the withdrawal of the reforms it had won and the reinvigoration of the system it had sought to reform. Alternatively, the movement could press ahead in the face of growing resistance from local and international capital that increasingly took the form, not just of economic sanctions, but also of efforts physically to destroy it. (Sometimes there is no choice: as the experience of the Popular Unity government in Chile in September 1973 shows, even a movement that tries to retreat can still be destroyed.) To press ahead would be, in effect, to undertake a revolution: in other words, the intensity of establishment resistance to significant reform makes the only stable outcomes once a partial break in the logic of capital has taken place either the reversal of these reforms (and perhaps a counter-revolution that turns the clock significantly further back, as did, for example, the neo-liberal reaction to the upheavals of the 1960s and early 1970s) or the introduction of a completely different social logic – a revolution, in other words. But the latter option would be a revolution not simply in the sense of a systemic transformation: it could only be achieved by overcoming – forcibly if necessary – the resistance of capital and of those it mobilized behind it. A movement that followed this path could only succeed by winning the active support of the majority of the population, particularly with the reserves of collective strength that only the organized working class possesses, and by appealing to the solidarity of like-minded movements around the world.

Susan George is not alone when, in a passage I cited in the previous chapter, she imagines revolution as the accompaniment of the 'global accident', a catastrophic economic collapse that would bring in its wake appalling suffering. But there are other ways of thinking about revolution. One might see it instead as an extension of democratic processes of self-government that developed initially through partial attempts to combat the excesses of the market. These processes could emerge in a variety of ways: as a result of government reforms extracted by popular movements; as forms of self-organization initially created more effectively to prosecute mass struggles from below; and as means of coping with a catastrophic deterioration in the material situation of the mass of population, as in the case of contemporary Argentina (which does seem like a national version of the 'global accident'). The revolutionary choice is really this: should these democratic forms of self-organization progressively take over the management of the economy, in order to replace the logic of capital with the claims of need, or should they limit themselves to serving as a humane supplement to the market, in which case all historical experience suggests that the two logics cannot indefinitely coexist and that the empire of the market will, sooner or later re-establish itself? If neither side holds back then, sooner or later, a decisive test of strength is unavoidable. To undertake a revolutionary project today, at the beginning of the twenty-first century, is an awesome task, particularly given the destructive power that the lords of capital now command. It is, however, the path on which the anti-capitalist movement has embarked – not as a result of a conscious strategy but through the logic of the struggles in which it is engaged. But the alternative seems to be to give up any aspiration even to the partial reform of the present system. If this dilemma is a real one, then – for all the potential risks and costs involved in the revolutionary project – it seems to be the only option open to anyone not content to acquiesce in the injustice, suffering, and destruction to which the present system has condemned the world.

Summary

- The values implicit in the global movement's critique of capitalism are justice, efficiency, democracy, and sustainability;
- These values are inconsistent with a market economy in Polanyi's sense – that is, an economic system governed by the self-regulating market;
- Neither of the most widely supported strategies for humanizing the market – market socialism and a more regulated version of capitalism – is likely to work;
- A democratically planned socialist economy – perhaps along the lines of Pat Devine's model of negotiated coordination – offers the best hope of realizing the values of the anti-capitalist movement;
- More immediately, it is possible to develop a programme of reforms that are both desirable in themselves and challenge the logic of capital: though these demands are mainly directed at the nation-state, they could only be pursued as part of an international movement and won through mass struggles;
- The struggle for such changes would, in all probability, evoke such resistance from capital as to confront the movement with a choice between abandoning its existing achievements and prosecuting a revolutionary challenge to the present system.

Afterword

Globalization is a good example of what W. B. Gallie called an essentially contested concept.[1] It is contested along two dimensions – explanatory and normative. That is, there is a debate about the nature and extent of globalization, and there is also a debate about whether it is, as *1066 and All That* would put it, a Good Thing. There is no reason why the position that one takes along one dimension should correspond to that taken along the other. For example, many in the anti-capitalist movement accept some of the more extreme factual claims about globalization, but condemn it morally and politically.[2]

If we take first the explanatory dimension of the globalization debate, we have, on the one hand, the claim that an irreversible shift has taken place in the direction of global economic, political, and cultural integration whose tendency is to abolish borders and make nation-states irrelevant. This is asserted by boosters of globalization such as Ken Ohmae and by critics such as Noreena Hertz. Particularly among the boosters there is a strong tendency towards teleology, that is, towards presenting globalization as an end-state towards which the world is inevitably tending. Advocates of the Third Way are particularly prone to suggesting that opposing globalization is as silly as resisting the weather (perhaps not as helpful an analogy as it might seem given the role that human actions are playing in causing climate change). Even the much more nuanced and sophisticated analysis of globalization offered by David Held, Anthony McGrew and their collaborators portrays it as a trans-historical process.[3]

On the other hand, the sceptics see globalization as a much more contingent and reversible process. Analysts writing from various political perspectives – for example, the revolutionary left (Chris Harman), traditional social democracy (Paul Hirst and Grahame Thompson), liberal internationalism (Robert Gilpin), and the Tory right (Niall Ferguson) – have all pointed out that the trends towards global economic integration over the past generation look less impressive when they are compared, not with the first half of the twentieth century, but with the end of the nineteenth century, when international trade and investment reached levels relative to national income that were not to be matched till the last quarter-century.[4] The implication of this argument is that there is nothing unprecedented about contemporary economic globalization, and that, moreover, it may not be sustained.

The distinguished economic historian Harold James reacted to the challenge thrown down to capitalist globalization by the Seattle protests by considering the historical precedent provided by 'the collapse of globalism in the inter-war depression'. He argues that the disintegration of the world economy in the early 1930s – precipitated by financial instability bearing marked similarities to the panics of the past decade – created the conditions in which the resentments caused by the first wave of globalization (1870–1914) could find political expression in a nationalist reaction: protectionism, restrictions on immigration, and, of course, autarkic regimes such as National Socialism in Germany and Stalinism in the Soviet Union. 'The Age of Nationalism' supplanted 'the Age of Capital', leading to a terrible world war. Considering the contem-

porary backlash against globalization from the perspective
of liberal internationalism, James argues that it lacks intellectual coherence and the kind of apparently successful
alternative economic model provided in the 1930s particularly by the Soviet Five-Year Plans. But he concludes: 'The
absence of these two features . . . explains why the pen-
dulum is so slow to swing back from globality. But it does
not and cannot explain why it will not swing.'[5]

James's historical comparison leads us immediately to
the normative dimension of the debate on globalization.
He presents contemporary opposition to globalization as
necessarily nationalist: 'At present there is the beginning
of an anti-globalist coalition, based on hostility to immigration (because of concerns about the labour market),
a belief in capital controls (in order to prevent shocks
emanating from the financial sector), and scepticism about
global trade.'[6] Now there undoubtedly is nationalist opposition to the contemporary forms of globalization. Third
World leaders such as Mahatir Mohamed of Malaysia and
Robert Mugabe of Zimbabwe have emerged as nationalist critics of the Washington Consensus in recent years.
Mahatir reacted to the Asian crisis of 1997–8 by reintroducing capital controls that allowed the Malaysian
economy to ride out the crisis relatively easily. Mugabe's
opposition to neo-liberalism is much more opportunistic:
his reversion to anti-colonial rhetoric was primarily a
response to the social and political rebellion provoked by
structural adjustment policies that his own government
had imposed at the IMF's behest in the early 1990s. There
are nationalist opponents of globalization in the North as
well: in chapter 2 I discussed the phenomenon of reactionary anti-capitalism represented, for example, by European fascism and the populist right in the United States.

It is, however, nonsense to claim that what is called (mis-
leadingly) the anti-globalization movement is nationalist.
Quite apart from the movement's international character,
on the issue of asylum and refugees it is well to the left of
the official consensus. It is governments committed to cor-

porate globalization that have frequently suspended international agreements and closed their borders to protesters from other countries. The Call of the Social Movements adopted at Porto Alegre II in February 2002 demands 'the right of free movement, the right to physical integrity and legal status of all migrants'. Even those on the reformist wing of the anti-capitalist movement who seek the reassertion of national sovereignty tend to view this as a step towards a less hierarchical and more pluralist world system. Daniel Bensaïd is therefore right to describe the anti-capitalist movement as an 'internationalist renewal':

> By comparison with the Second or the Third International, the internationalism of the twenty-first century straightaway reveals a really planetary dimension. Responding to the generalized commodification and privatization of the world, it is more extended and more geographically varied than its predecessors, and also more complex. It must combine cultures and gather together a diversity of actors irreducible to the traditional workers' movement on its own: feminist, ecological, and cultural movements, youth campaigns and trade unions. Hardly recovered from the traumatic experiences of the twentieth century, it emerges cautiously [avec prudence]. For the politics of the oppressed are not free of the disillusionments and of the defeats accumulated by the 'Age of Extremes'.[7]

The prudence that Bensaïd describes is real enough. It reflects the fact that the movement against capitalist globalization developed in what appeared to be an ideological vacuum, but what was in reality the artificially homogeneous intellectual climate created by the very defeats and disillusionments to which Bensaïd refers and by the apparent triumph of liberal capitalism after 1989. Hence the confusion about what to call the movement. Hence also the more substantive ambiguities about strategies and alternatives that I have highlighted in this book. Bensaïd argues that Porto Alegre II 'perhaps marked the apogee of the first consensual wave of anti-globalization. The

events intervening since the attacks on New York on 11
September 2001 . . . put onto the agenda questions whose
political implications, without going as far as breaking the
unity, bring powerful tensions to the heart of the movement
of resistance to liberal globalization'.[8] I have tried to
address these questions in a way that can contribute to the
further development of a movement whose logic is to challenge the very existence of the capitalist mode of production. My conclusion is that this movement can succeed only
through a revolutionary transformation that establishes a
new global economic system based upon social ownership
of the main productive resources and democratic planning.

But I wish finally to return to the question of the values
that such a transformation might seek to realize. 'Values'
are constantly invoked in the dominant discourse. Celebrating what it mistakenly believed to be the decline of the
anti-capitalist movement after 9–11, the *Financial Times*
claimed to perceive 'a sharply reduced appetite since September 11 for fundamental attacks on the values underlying the US and other western industrialized countries'.[9]
These values presumably define the 'civilized world' that
has constantly been portrayed as the protagonist in the
'war on terrorism'. George W. Bush told the Palestinian
people in April 2002: 'everyone must choose; you're with
the civilized world, or you're with the terrorists.'[10]

Observing the death and destruction that the Israel
Defence Force inflicted on the West Bank and Gaza in
the name of 'fighting terrorism', many people around the
world must have recalled Gandhi's famous reply when
asked what he thought of Western civilization: 'It would
be a good idea.' But one can take such establishment
pronouncements a little more seriously, and consider what
these 'civilized values' are – the values of Western liberal
capitalist societies. The most obvious candidates are the
slogans of the Great French Revolution – liberty, equality,
and fraternity, or, as we might now prefer to call it, solidarity. But these too are all essentially contested concepts.[11] In contemporary political philosophy, New Right

theorists such as the late Robert Nozick have bitterly opposed the reading of central liberal values given by egalitarians such as John Rawls. Neo-liberalism – the ideology of the Washington Consensus that underlies the Bush administration's war drive – offers a highly selective realization of these values. It reduces freedom to the right to buy and sell and equality to a legal form, disintegrates solidarity into privatized individualism, and threatens the very planet on which all humans depend to realize their desires and pursue their projects. The anti-capitalist movement offers a radically different reading of liberty, equality, and solidarity, according to which their realization can only be achieved against, and (I argue) through the replacement of global capitalism. It is this movement that bears the real promise of modernity by promoting a genuinely universal emancipation that would make the fate of the planet and those on it a collective and democratic project. Now more than ever, we have a world to win.

Notes

Introduction

1 F. Fukuyama, *The End of History and the Last Man* (New York, 1992). For a critical discussion of Fukuyama's thesis and the debate it provoked, see A. Callinicos, *Theories and Narratives* (Cambridge, 1995), ch. 1.

2 For a recent critique of this argument, see S. Žižek, *Did Somebody Say Totalitarianism?* (London, 2001).

3 See R. Broad and J. Cavanaugh, 'The Death of the Washington Consensus?', in W. Bello et al., eds, *Global Finance* (London, 2000), p. 84.

4 S. George, 'A Short History of Neo-liberalism', ibid., p. 27.

5 This story is told, primarily from a Third World perspective, in W. Bello et al., *Dark Victory: The United States and World Poverty* (2nd edn, London, 1999).

6 See especially P. Gowan, *The Global Gamble* (London, 1999).

7 J. R. MacArthur, *The Selling of 'Free Trade'* (Berkeley and Los Angeles, 2000).

8 A. Callinicos, *Against the Third Way* (Cambridge, 2001).

9 P. Anderson, 'Renewals', *New Left Review*, (II) 1 (2000), p. 17. See Gilbert Achcar's measured critique, 'The "Historical Pessimism" of Perry Anderson', *International Socialism*, (2) 88 (2000).

10 Compare M. Wolf, 'In Defence of Global Capitalism', *Financial Times*, 8 December 1999 and F. Rouleau, 'L'Ennemi, est-ce la "mondialisation" ou le capitalisme?', *Lutte Ouvrière*, 3 December 1999.

11 J. Harding, 'Globalization's Children Strike Back', *Financial Times*, 11 September 2001. For more sympathetic surveys, see, for example, A. Starr, *Naming the Enemy: Anti-Corporate Movements Confront Globalization* (London, 2000), and E. Bircham and G. Charlton, eds, *Anti-Capitalism: A Guide to the Movement* (London, 2001). Daniel Bensaïd has written a fine overview (2002) in 'Le Nouvel internationalisme', forthcoming in *Encyclopaedia Universalis*.

12 M. Rupert, *Ideologies of Globalization* (London, 2000), pp. 15, 70.

13 'Testimonies of the First Day', in T. Hayden, ed., *The Zapatista Reader* (New York, 2002), p. 216.

14 Subcommandante Marcos, 'The Fourth World War has Begun', ibid., p. 273.

15 J. Lloyd, *The Protest Ethic* (London, 2001), pp. 38–9.

16 A. Pettifor, 'The Economic Bondage of Debt – and the Birth of a New Movement', *New Left Review*, (I) 230 (1998).

17 See P. Bond, 'Their Reforms and Ours', in Bello et al., eds, *Global Finance*, and R. Wade, 'Showdown at the World Bank', *New Left Review*, (II) 7 (2001). Liberal internationalist perspectives on these debates are offered in R. Gilpin, *The Challenge of Global Capitalism* (Princeton, 2000) and H. James, *The End of Globalization* (Cambridge MA, 2001). Stiglitz has now developed his critique of the IMF in particular in *Globalization and Its Discontents* (London, 2002).

18 J. Wolfreys, 'Class Struggles in France', *International Socialism*, (2) 84 (1999).

19 L. Boltanski and E. Chapiello, *Le Nouvel esprit de capitalisme* (Paris, 1999), esp. Part III.

20 J. Baudrillard, *The Illusion of the End* (Cambridge, 1994), p. 81.

21 G. Debord, *The Society of the Spectacle* (Detroit, 1970), §§ 1, 2.

22 Boltanski and Chapiello, *Le Nouvel esprit de capitalisme*, p. 548. Boltanski and Chapiello go on, rather oddly, to associate Bourdieu with the critique of authenticity, even though,

as they acknowledge, the concept continues to play a role in his thought: see ibid., pp. 549–50 and 769, n. 39.

23 See, for example, J. Baudrillard, *Simulations* (New York, 1983): the Situationist analysis is explicitly rejected on p. 54.

24 R. Rorty, *Achieving Our Country* (Cambridge MA, 1998), pp. 73–107.

25 See especially S. Žižek, *The Ticklish Subject* (London, 1999).

26 N. Klein, *No Logo* (London, 2000), pp. 122, 124.

27 N. Klein, 'Reclaiming the Commons', *New Left Review*, (II) 9 (2001), p. 87.

28 S. George, 'Que faire à present?', text for the first World Social Forum, Porto Alegre, 15 January 2001.

29 Speech at the second World Social Forum, Porto Alegre, 1 February 2002.

30 R. Falk, 'The Making of Global Citizenship', in J. Brecher et al., eds, *Global Visions* (Boston, 1993), p. 39.

31 G. Arrighi et al., *Anti-Systemic Movements* (London, 1989).

32 Speech at the second World Social Forum, Porto Alegre, 2 February 2002. The development of this kind of activism is one of the main themes of Paul Ginsborg's *Italy and its Discontents* (London, 2002), although he fails to anticipate its recent radicalization.

33 M. Cooper, 'Street Fight in Seattle', *The Nation*, 20 December 1999 (online version).

34 'Porto Alegre II: Call of the Social Movements', 4 February 2002, www.resist.org.

35 *Financial Times*, 6 October 2001. The conclusion to the series (in the event only two parts were published in the paper, although it is available in its entirety online at www.specials.ft.com/countercap) paints a similarly downbeat picture: J. Harding, 'Clamour against Capitalism Stilled', ibid., 10 October 2001.

36 Lloyd, *Protest Ethic*, pp. 66–7.

37 Tariq Ali offers a robust critique of such illusions in *The Clash of Fundamentalisms* (London, 2002).

38 *Financial Times*, 18 March 2002.

39 C. Serfati, *La Mondialisation armée* (Paris, 2001).

40 G. Monbiot, 'World Bank to West Bank', *Guardian*, 9 April 2002.

41 I am also indebted to Chris Harman's pioneering analysis, 'Anti-Capitalism: Theory and Practice', *International Socialism*, (2) 88 (2000).

Chapter 1   Capitalism Against the Planet

1 N. Hertz, *The Silent Takeover* (London, 2001), p. 10.
2 *Financial Times*, 1 November 2001.
3 *Independent*, 30 November 1999.
4 See, for example, A. Sen, *Development as Freedom* (Oxford, 1999).
5 *Guardian*, 18 January 2002. For further discussion, see A. Callinicos, *Equality* (Cambridge, 2000).
6 M. Weisbrot et al., 'The Scorecard on Globalization 1980–2000: Twenty Years of Diminished Progress', 18 August 2001, www.cepr.net, pp. 1–2.
7 J. Weeks, 'Globalize, Globa-lize, Global Lies: Myths of the World Economy in the 1990s', in R. Albritton et al., *Phases of Capitalist Development* (Houndmills, 2001), pp. 272–3. Even William Easterly of the World Bank has acknowledged the 'significant puzzle' that, despite neo-liberal 'policy reforms' that 'should have led to accelerating, not falling growth', median per capita growth in the developing countries declined from 2.5 per cent a year in 1960–79 to zero per cent in 1980–99: 'The Lost Decades: Developing Countries' Stagnation in Spite of Policy Reform', *Journal of Economic Growth* 6 (2001), p. 154.
8 J. Stiglitz, 'Lessons from Argentina's Debacle', *Sand in the Wheels*, 113, 16 January 2002, www.attac.org.
9 *Financial Times*, 2 January 2002.
10 This view of a world-historical struggle between different variants of capitalism is powerfully articulated in M. Albert, *Capitalism against Capitalism* (London, 1993).
11 For a vivid portrayal of this coalition at work in Britain, see G. Monbiot, *Captive State* (London, 2000).
12 Other radical cultural theorists such as Walter Benjamin, Gilles Deleuze, Pierre Macherey, and Raymond Williams, perhaps less attached than Adorno and Horkheimer to the Romantic conception of the artist as a creative individual, had no qualms about conceiving art and literature as processes of production, but it is doubtful that they had in

mind anything resembling *Big Brother* or *Who Wants to be a Millionaire?*

13 Subcommandante Marcos, 'The Fourth World War has Begun', in T. Hayden, ed., *The Zapatista Reader* (New York, 2002), p. 275.

14 W. Bello et al., 'Notes on the Ascendancy and Regulation of Speculative Capital', in Bello et al, eds, *Global Finance* (London, 2000), p. 4. There is an interesting discussion of the significance of financial capitalism in G. Duménil et al., *Une nouvelle phase de capitalisme?* (Paris, 2001).

15 Heikki Patomäki has provided a particularly systematic statement of this case in *Democratizing Globalization* (London, 2001).

16 J. Grahl, 'Globalized Finance', *New Left Review*, (II) 8 (2001), p. 31.

17 Ibid., p. 34. The Clinton administration's brush with the bond market is discussed in A. Callinicos, *Against the Third Way* (Cambridge, 2001), pp. 23–6.

18 Grahl, 'Globalized Finance', pp. 40–1.

19 C. Harman, 'Beyond the Boom', *International Socialism*, (2) 90 (2001) and R. Brenner, *The Boom and the Bubble* (London, 2002).

20 K. Marx, *Capital*, III (Harmondsworth, 1981), p. 969 (translation modified).

21 I say 'partly' because financial actors gained power also as a result of the collapse of the Bretton Woods system, a process that had independent economic causes (the decline of US competitiveness relative to Japan and West Germany), but one in which financial markets themselves played a role, through, for example, speculating against or for different currencies (respectively, the dollar and the pound sterling, and the yen and the Deutschmark). For an overview, see F. Block, *The Origins of International Economic Disorder* (Berkeley and Los Angeles, 1977).

22 P. Gowan, *The Global Gamble* (London, 1999).

23 S. Damodaran, 'Capital Account Convertibility', in Bello et al., eds, *Global Finance*.

24 Patomäki, *Democratizing Globalization*, p. 31.

25 R. Blackburn, 'The Enron Debacle and the Pension Crisis', *New Left Review*, (II) 14 (2002), p. 29. See also W. Greider, 'Crime in the Suites', *The Nation*, 4 February 2002.

26 Quoted in Bello et al., 'Notes on the Ascendancy and Regulation of Speculative Capital', p. 16.

27 Quoted in R. J. Shiller, *Irrational Exuberance* (Princeton, 2001), p. 172.

28 J. E. Stiglitz and A. Weiss, 'Credit Rationing in Markets with Perfect Information', *American Economic Review*, 71 (1981), p. 409. Moreover: ' "Efficient market" theorists state that costless information is a *sufficient* condition for prices to fully reflect all information . . . They are not aware that it is a necessary condition as well. But this is a *reductio ad absurdum*, since prices are important only when information is costly,' S. J. Grossman and J. E. Stiglitz, 'Information and Competitive Price Systems', ibid., 66 (1976), p. 248. See also, *inter alia*, B. Greenwald et al., 'Informational Imperfection in the Capital Market and Macroeconomic Fluctuations', ibid., 74 (1984).

29 J. M. Keynes, *The General Theory of Employment Interest and Money* (London, 1970), ch. 12.

30 M. Kidron, *Western Capitalism since the War* (Harmondsworth, 1970), and C. Harman, *Explaining the Crisis* (London, 1984), ch. 3.

31 J. Tobin [1978], 'A Proposal for Monetary Reform', reprinted as an appendix to Patomäki, *Democratizing Globalization*, pp. 234, 240.

32 D. Felix and R. Sau, 'On the Revenue Potential and Phasing in of the Tobin Tax', in M. ul Haq et al., eds, *The Tobin Tax* (New York, 1996), p. 236. Others favour a lower rate: Patomäki, for example, proposes 0.05 or 0.1 per cent (*Democratizing Globalization*, pp. 141ff.). Tobin himself was much less interested in his tax as a mechanism of redistribution – see, for example, his 'Prologue' to ul Haq et al., *Tobin Tax*, p. xvi.

33 Tobin, 'Proposal', p. 239.

34 Patomäki, *Democratizing Globalization*, p. 220.

35 I am indebted for the vertical/horizontal contrast to Robert Brenner: see 'The Economics of Global Turbulence', *New Left Review*, (I) 229 (1998), p. 23. My interpretation of Marx's *Capital* was first published in *Is There a Future for Marxism?* (London, 1982). Good treatments will be found in R. Rosdolsky, *The Making of Marx's 'Capital'* (London, 1977), J. Weeks, *Capital and Exploitation*

(London, 1981), and J. Bidet, *Que faire du Capital?* (Paris, 1985).

36 For further discussion of this point, see Callinicos, *Equality*, esp. ch. 3.

37 The parasitism of capital relative to the creativity of the 'multitude' is one of the main themes of M. Hardt and A. Negri, *Empire* (Cambridge MA, 2000).

38 See esp. Marx, *Capital*, III, Part 3. The forces and relations of production and the other main concepts of historical materialism are discussed in L. Althusser and E. Balibar, *Reading Capital* (London, 1970), G. A. Cohen, *Karl Marx's Theory of History* (Oxford, 1978), and A. Callinicos, *Making History* (Cambridge, 1987).

39 For some contrasting Marxist accounts, see Harman, *Explaining the Crisis*, P. Armstrong et al., *Capitalism since World War II* (London, 1984), G. Duménil and D. Lévy, *La Dynamique du capital* (Paris, 1996), and Brenner, 'The Economics of Global Turbulence'.

40 For a survey of the controversy, see S. Cullenberg, *The Falling Rate of Profit* (New York, 1994).

41 *Financial Times*, 17 June 1997.

42 Robert Brenner offers a detailed analysis of this process in *The Boom and the Bubble*. Underlying this analysis is an unorthodox Marxist theory of crisis, first developed in 'The Economics of Global Turbulence', and extensively criticized in a symposium in *Historical Materialism*, 4 and 5 (1999).

43 Brenner, *The Boom and the Bubble*, ch. 7.

44 The dissident British economist Wynne Godley has highlighted this process in a series of papers since the late 1990s: for the latest, see W. Godley and A. Izurieta, 'As the Implosion Begins . . . ?', July 2001, www.levy.org.

45 *Financial Times*, 3 August 2001.

46 Ibid., 23 January 2002.

47 For a critical restatement of the Marxist theory of money and credit, see M. Itoh and C. Lapavitsas, *Political Economy of Money and Finance* (London, 1999).

48 J. R. McNeill, *Something New Under the Sun* (London, 2000), pp. xx, xxi.

49 Sen, *Development as Freedom*, ch. 9.

50 McNeill, *Something New Under the Sun*, pp. 296–7.

51 Ibid., p. 313.

52 Ibid., p. 332.

53 F. Engels, *Dialectics of Nature* (Moscow, 1972), pp. 179, 180. Engels's relationship to nature was *sui generis*, at least for a socialist: on the previous page he cites observations of fox behaviour obtained while hunting.

54 For three excellent recent treatments, see P. Burkett, *Marx and Nature* (New York, 1999), J. Bellamy Foster, *Marx's Ecology* (New York, 2000) and J. Hughes, *Ecology and Historical Materialism* (Cambridge, 2000).

55 For Marxist interpretations of Stalinism, see, among a vast literature, L. D. Trotsky, *The Revolution Betrayed* (New York, 1970), T. Cliff, *State Capitalism in Russia* (rev. edn, London, 1988), and A. Callinicos, *The Revenge of History* (Cambridge, 1991).

56 P. McGarr, 'Why Green is Red', *International Socialism*, (2) 88 (2000).

57 M. Davis, *Late Victorian Holocausts* (London, 2001): quotations from pp. 15 and 288. Davis also explores the destructive interaction between natural processes and the capitalist model of development in *Ecology of Fear* (New York, 1998).

58 See, for example, the rise and fall of the civilization of Easter Island, described by Clive Ponting in the opening chapter of *A Green History of the World* (Harmondsworth, 1993).

59 S. George, 'Que faire à present?', text for the first World Social Forum, Porto Alegre, 15 January 2001.

60 George W. Bush, 'Address to a Joint Session of Congress and the American People', 20 September 2001, www.whitehouse.gov. See A. Giddens, *The Third Way* (Cambridge, 1998), pp. 70–8.

61 T. L. Friedman, *The Lexus and the Olive Tree* (London, 2000), p. 464.

62 *Financial Times*, 18 February 2002.

63 P. Kennedy, *The Rise and Fall of the Great Powers* (London, 1989), pp. 665–6. For a shrewd contemporary critique, see J. S. Nye, Jr, *Bound to Lead* (New York, 1991).

64 Idem, 'The Eagle Has Landed', *Financial Times*, 2 February 2002.

65 Hardt and Negri, *Empire*, pp. xii, 190. For a critique of *Empire*, see A. Callinicos, 'Toni Negri in Perspective', *International Socialism*, (2) 92 (2001).

66 T. Negri, 'Ruptures dans l'empire, puissance de l'exode', 27 October 2001, interview in *Multitudes*, 7 (online version), multitudes-infos@samizdat.net.

67 See, for example, D. Held, A. McGrew et al., *Global Transformations* (Cambridge, 1999), and for a critique, Callinicos, *Against the Third Way*, ch. 3.

68 R. Cooper [2002], 'Reordering the World', www.fpc.org.uk and www.observer.co.uk.

69 Tacitus, *Agricola*, 30.

70 C. Johnson, *Blowback: The Costs and Consequences of American Empire* (New York, 2000), pp. 205, 213.

71 Ibid., pp. 8, 33.

72 Ibid., p. 224.

73 See A. Callinicos et al., *Marxism and the New Imperialism* (London, 1984); A. Callinicos, 'Periodizing Capitalism and Analysing Imperialism', in Albritton et al., eds, *Phases of Capitalist Development*; and idem, 'Marxism and Global Governance', in D. Held and A. McGrew, eds, *Governing Globalization* (Cambridge, 2002).

74 For a historical overview of this process, see E. J. Hobsbawm, *The Age of Capital 1848–1875* (London, 1975), and *The Age of Empire 1875–1914* (London, 1987).

75 See, for example, G. Arrighi, 'World Income Inequalities and the Future of Socialism', *New Left Review*, (I) 189 (1991).

76 M. Mann, 'Globalization and September 11', *New Left Review*, (II) 12 (2001), p. 54.

77 Three critical Marxist perspectives on Third World development are provided by R. Brenner, 'The Origins of Capitalist Development', *New Left Review*, (I) 104 (1977), N. Harris, *The End of the Third World* (London, 1986), and C. Harman, 'Where is Capitalism Going?', II, *International Socialism*, (2) 60 (1993).

78 See, for example, C. Harman, 'The State and Capitalism Today', *International Socialism*, (2) 51 (1991) and W. Bonefeld, ed., *The Politics of Europe* (Houndmills, 2001).

79 For example, P. Gowan, 'The Euro-Atlantic Origins of NATO's Attack on Yugoslavia', in T. Ali, ed., *Masters of the Universe?* (London, 2000).

80 S. P. Huntington, 'The Lonely Superpower', *Foreign Affairs*, March/April 1999 (online edition), www.foreignpolicy2000.org.

81 C. Rice, 'Campaign 2000 – Promoting the National Interest', *Foreign Affairs*, January/February 2000 (online edition), www.foreignpolicy2000.org.

82 Quoted in Johnson, *Blowback*, p. 217.

83 Huntington, 'The Lonely Superpower'. Perry Anderson stresses the continuities between the Clinton and younger Bush administrations in 'Testing Formula Two', *New Left Review*, (II) 8 (2001).

84 Z. Brzezinski, *The Grand Chessboard* (New York, 1997).

85 See also J. Rees, 'Imperialism: Globalization, the State and War', *International Socialism*, (2) 93 (2001), and D. Bensaïd, 'Dieu, que ces guerres sont saintes!', *ContreTemps*, 3 (2002).

86 'The President's State of the Union Address', 29 January 2002, www.whitehouse.gov.

87 J. Bolton, 'Beyond the Axis of Evil', 6 May 2002, www.state.gov.

88 N. Lemann, 'The Next World Order', *The New Yorker*, 1 April 2002 (online edition), www.newyorker.com.

89 *Guardian*, 8 March 2002.

90 W. M. Arkin, 'Secret Plan Outlines the Unthinkable', *Los Angeles Times*, 10 March 2002.

91 United States Space Command, *Vision for 2020*, February 1997, www.spacecom.af.mil/usspace.

92 For much more analysis of the relationship between economic and military globalization, see C. Serfati, *La Mondialisation armée* (Paris, 2001).

Chapter 2   *Varieties and Strategies*

1 For a sympathetic account, see R. Sayre and M. Löwy, 'Figures of Romantic Anti-Capitalism', *New German Critique*, 32 (1984). Quite distinct from the racist and authoritarian populism discussed in this sub-section is the more straightforwardly conservative critique of globalization put forward, for example, by John Gray. While sharing many of the criticisms of the Washington Consensus made by Soros, Stiglitz, et al., Gray argues that neo-liberalism, like Marxism, is a version of Enlightenment rationalism that seeks to impose a universal civilization: *False Dawn* (London, 1999). Edward Luttwak is another, more interest-

ing conservative critic of globalization: see, for example, *Turbo-Capitalism* (London, 1999).

2 Z. Sternhell, *Ni droite ni gauche* (3rd edn; Brussels, 2000), p. 138.

3 M. Rupert, *Ideologies of Globalization* (London, 2000), p. 95; see generally ibid., ch. 5.

4 Ibid., p. 97. Ideologies are nevertheless frequently ambiguous. As Rupert notes, anti-globalization populism can sometimes prove itself open to a more structural and cosmopolitan critique: ibid., ch. 6. One of the main themes of Sternhell's study is the way in which French fascism drew heavily on disillusioned leftists for its leaders, who occasionally returned to the left: see, for example, *Ni droite ni gauche*, ch. III, for the case of Georges Valois, the ex-syndicalist who founded the first fascist movement in France but died a victim of Nazism in Belsen.

5 Sternhell, *Ni droite ni gauche*, p. 139.

6 H. A. Turner, Jr, *German Big Business and the Rise of Hitler* (New York, 1985), p. 76.

7 A. Callinicos, 'Plumbing the Depths: Marxism and the Holocaust', *The Yale Journal of Criticism*, 14 (2001).

8 K. Marx and F. Engels, *The Communist Manifesto* (London, 1998), p. 70.

9 N. Hertz, *The Silent Takeover* (London, 2001), p. 10.

10 N. Hertz, 'Trojan Horse at the Feast of Globalization', *Observer*, 10 February 2002.

11 Hertz, *Silent Takeover*, p. 11.

12 Ibid., pp. 188, 204, 212.

13 I am indebted for this point to Sam Ashman. For a critique of the thesis, see L. Weiss, *The Myth of the Powerless State* (Cambridge, 1998).

14 R. Cowe, 'The Respectable Face of Anti-Capitalism', *Observer*, 6 May 2001.

15 R. Tomkins, 'When Caring is a Good Investment', *Financial Times*, 5 October 2001.

16 J. Harding, 'Feeding the Hands that Bite', 15 October 2001, www.specials.ft.com/countercap.

17 D. James, 'Fair Trade, Not Free Trade', in K. Danaher and R. Burbach, eds, *Globalize This!* (Monroe, ME, 2000), p. 189. See also D. Ransom, *The No-Nonsense Guide to Fair Trade* (London, 2001).

18 C. Hines, *Localization: A Global Manifesto* (London, 2000), p. viii.

19 G. Monbiot, 'Land, Genes and Justice', *Imprints*, 3:2 (1998–9), and *Captive State* (London, 2000).

20 Hines, *Localization*, Part 3 (quotation from p. 80).

21 K. Marx, *Capital*, I (Harmondsworth, 1976), p. 181, n. 4. Marx's most detailed critique of Proudhonist economics is to be found in *Grundrisse* (Harmondsworth, 1973), esp. pp. 115–56, 239–50.

22 Hines, *Localization*, p. 263.

23 P. Bond, 'Their Reforms and Ours', in W. Bello et al., eds, *Global Finance* (London, 2000), pp. 66–7.

24 J. Tobin, 'Prologue', in M. ul Haq et al., eds, *The Tobin Tax* (New York, 1996), p. xiii.

25 W. Bello, 'Reforming the WTO is the Wrong Agenda', in Danaher and Burbach, eds, *Globalize This!*, pp. 117–18.

26 H. Patomäki, *Democratizing Globalization* (London, 2001): figures on p. 164.

27 K. Malhotra, 'Renewing the Governance of the Global Economy', in Bello et al., eds, *Global Finance*, p. 59.

28 S. George, 'Clusters of Crisis and a Planetary Contract', *Sand in the Wheels*, 21 November 2001, www.attac.org.

29 For example, A. MacEwan, 'Argentine: The IMF Strikes Back', ibid., 16 January 2002, and J. Brecher et al., 'Two, Three, Many Argentinas?', 17 January 2002, www.villageorpillage.org.

30 S. George, 'Que faire à présent?', text for the first World Social Forum, Porto Alegre, 15 January 2001.

31 See, for a critical analysis of Negri's thought that traces its roots to the autonomist movement of the 1970s, A. Callinicos, 'Toni Negri in Perspective', *International Socialism*, (2) 92 (2001), and, for a history of autonomist Marxism, S. Wright, *Storming Heaven* (London, 2002).

32 Autonomism shades off into more traditional forms of anarchism, represented notably by Michael Albert: for example, 'Anarchism', in E. Bircham and J. Charlton, eds, *Anti-Capitalism: A Guide to the Movement* (London, 2001). See also D. Graeber, 'For a New Anarchism', *New Left Review*, (II) 13 (2002).

33 N. Klein, 'The Vision Thing', 10 July 2000, *The Nation* (online edition), www.thenation.com.

34 It is a matter of controversy whether this concern for the interests of the indigenous peoples was central to EZLN strategy from the start of their rising in January 1994 or represented a subsequent adaptation to an unfavourable military balance of forces. For two sympathetic but critical appraisals of the EZLN, see J. Mancillas, 'The Twilight of the Revolutionaries' and M. Gonzalez, 'The Zapatistas: The Challenges of Revolution in a New Millennium', both in T. Hayden, ed., *The Zapatista Reader* (New York, 2002).

35 Subcommandante Marcos, 'Of Trees, Crimes, and Odontology', in ibid., p. 267. See also Naomi Klein's enthusiastic piece on Marcos, 'The Unknown Icon', in ibid.

36 Subcommandante Marcos, 'The Fourth World War Has Begun', in ibid., p. 283. This text was indeed originally published in *Le Monde diplomatique*.

37 M. Hardt and A. Negri, *Empire* (Cambridge MA, 2000), p. 133. See more generally, ibid., chs. 2.2 and 2.3.

38 F. Barchiesi et al., 'Porto Alegre 2002: The Work of the Multitude', multitudes-infos@samizdat.net.

39 N. Klein, 'Masochistic Capitalists', *Guardian*, 15 February 2002.

40 Speech at World Social Forum, Porto Alegre, 4 February 2002.

41 Barchiesi et al., 'Porto Alegre 2002'.

42 A. Callinicos, *The Anti-Capitalist Movement and the Revolutionary Left* (London, 2001) and D. Bensaïd, *Les Trotskysmes* (Paris, 2002).

43 P. Bond, 'Their Reforms and Ours', p. 69.

44 Ibid., p. 66.

45 J. Petras and H. Veltmeyer, *Globalization Unmasked* (Halifax, 2001), ch. 8.

46 See E. M. Wood, 'The Uses and Abuses of "Civil Society"', in R. Miliband and L. Panitch, eds, *Socialist Register 1990* (London, 1990).

47 See Alex de Waal's outstanding *Famine Crimes* (London, 1997).

48 See P. Cammack, 'Attacking the Poor', *New Left Review*, (II) 13 (2002).

49 W. Bello and N. Bullard, 'The Global Conjuncture: Characteristics and Challenges', *Focus on the Global South*, March 2001, www.focusweb.org.

50 *Financial Times*, 2 August 2001.
51 Ibid., 24 July 2001.
52 Ibid., 5 September 2001.
53 Ibid., 7 September 2001.
54 *Le Monde*, 5 February 2002. See also the eight-page supplement devoted to 'L'Autre Monde de Porto Alegre', ibid., 27 January 2002.
55 P. H. Gordon, 'Liberté! Fraternité! Anxiety!', *Financial Times*, 19 January 2002.
56 Klein, 'The Vision Thing'.
57 *Il Manifesto*, 3 August 2001.
58 See the various contributions to the symposium 'After Genoa – What Next?', *Socialist Review*, September 2001.
59 See, for example, the response by Bello's colleague Nicola Bullard, 'Bruised, Shaken but Defiant: Some Reflections on What Happened at Genoa', www.focusweb.org.
60 Speech at second World Social Forum, Porto Alegre, 2 February 2002. Bello's initial response to the Afghan War is to be found in 'The American War of War', December 2001, www.focusweb.org.
61 See esp. W. Bello et al., *Dark Victory: The US and Global Poverty* (2nd edn, London, 1999).
62 For the position of the ATTAC movements in Europe on the war in Afghanistan, see 'Contre le terrorisme, la justice et non pas la guerre', 10 November 2001, www.attac.org.
63 T. Negri, 'Ruptures dans l'empire, puissance de l'exode', 27 October 2001, *Multitudes*, no. 7, multitudes-infos@samizdat.net.
64 Hines, *Localization*, p. 72.
65 For a critique, see A. Callinicos, *Against Postmodernism* (Cambridge, 1989), ch. 5.
66 D. Filmer, 'Estimating the World at Work', WPS1488, 31 July 1995, www.worldbank.org.
67 A. Callinicos, *The Revolutionary Ideas of Karl Marx* (London, 1983), ch. 7.
68 See, for example, G. A. Cohen, *If You're an Egalitarian, How Come You're So Rich?* (Cambridge MA, 2000), esp. ch. 6, and my critical discussion of this book in 'Having Your Cake and Eating It', *Historical Materialism*, 9 (2001).
69 *Financial Times*, 1 May 2002.

70 A much more thorough analysis supporting this argument will be found in C. Harman, 'The Workers of the World', *International Socialism* (2) 96 (2002). Erik Olin Wright's careful analysis of contemporary American class structure in *Class Counts* (Cambridge, 1997) identifies some trends that apparently contradict this analysis – notably the relatively substantial growth of the entrepreneurial and salaried middle classes in the United States – that require further discussion, but these do not, in my opinion, invalidate the argument put here.

71 For more on this distinction between structure and collectivity, see A. Callinicos, *Making History* (Cambridge, 1987), chs 4 and 5.

72 See the literature discussed in A. Callinicos, *Equality* (Cambridge, 2000), ch. 3.

73 Interview with Charlie Kimber, December 1999.

74 K. Moody, 'Unions', in Bircham and Charlton, eds, *Anti-Capitalism*, p. 292.

75 See, for example, M. Hardt, 'Today's Bandung?', *New Left Review*, (II) 14 (2002), pp. 115–16.

76 C. Harman, 'Argentina: Rebellion at the Sharp End of the World Crisis', *International Socialism*, (2) 94 (2002), and 'Argentina After the Revolt: What Next?', *Socialist Worker*, 13 April 2002.

77 Interview in *Socialist Worker*, 20 April 2002.

78 'World Social Forum Charter of Principles', §9, www.forumsocialmundial.org.br.

79 Hardt, 'Today's Bandung', pp. 114, 117–18.

80 For all its ambiguities and the misappropriations to which it fell victim, Gramsci's thought remains the most important set of reflections on the political and ideological conditions of social transformation: see *Selections from the Prison Notebooks* (London, 1971).

81 See A. Callinicos, 'Unity in Diversity', *Socialist Review*, April 2002.

Chapter 3   Imagining Other Worlds

1 A. Callinicos, *Equality* (Cambridge, 2000). See also J. Roemer, *Theories of Distributive Justice* (Cambridge MA, 1996).

2 G. A. Cohen, *If You're an Egalitarian, How Come You're So Rich?* (Cambridge MA, 2000), chs 8 and 9.

3 J. Rawls, *The Law of Peoples* (Cambridge MA, 1999).

4 R. Dworkin, *Sovereign Virtue* (Cambridge MA, 2000).

5 D. Goldrej, *The No-Nonsense Guide to Climate Change* (London, 2001), p. 127.

6 C. R. Beitz, *Political Theory and International Relations* (rev. edn, Princeton, 1999), p. 176; see generally ibid., Part 3 and Afterword to the Revised Edition.

7 Some people on the left resist appeal to cosmopolitan principles because such principles have been used to justify Western military interventions, for example, against Yugoslavia in 1999: see, for example, D. Chandler, ' "International Justice" ', *New Left Review*, (II) 6 (2000). But an invalid inference from a true premiss to a false conclusion is not a reason for rejecting that premiss. The fundamental objection to Western interventions is that they maintain an unjust global order, not that they violate national sovereignty. For much more on the Yugoslav case, see T. Ali, ed., *Masters of the Universe?* (London, 2000).

8 See also G. A. Cohen, 'Incentives, Inequality, and Community', in G. B. Peterson, ed., *The Tanner Lectures on Human Values*, XIII (Salt Lake City, 1992).

9 See, for much broadly supporting argument, J. Hughes, *Ecology and Historical Materialism* (Cambridge, 2000), chs 5 and 6.

10 J. Bellamy Foster, *The Vulnerable Planet* (rev. edn, New York, 1999), p. 132.

11 See Goodrej, *No-Nonsense Guide to Climate Change*, ch. 7.

12 Subcommandante Marcos, 'The Fourth World War Has Begun', in T. Hayden, ed., *The Zapatista Reader* (New York, 2002), pp. 283–4.

13 For a forceful critique on some of the political implications of this outlook, see B. Barry, *Culture and Equality* (Cambridge, 2001).

14 See D. Bensaïd [2002], 'Le Nouvel internationalisme', forthcoming in *Encyclopaedia Universalis*.

15 Callinicos, *Equality*, pp. 79–87.

16 A. Sen, *Development as Freedom* (Oxford, 1999), p. 6. Sen put a version of this argument against the anti-capitalist protesters at the G8 summit in Genoa: *Guardian*, 19 July 2001.

17 For example, ibid., pp. 7, 29; see more generally ibid., ch. 5.
18 K. Marx, *Capital*, I (Harmondsworth, 1976), pp. 415–16 (the quoted phrase comes from an article by Engels). See also ibid., pp. 365, 377–8, where Marx compares capitalists' efforts to screw as much labour-time as possible out of their workers to slavery. Marx discusses the economic superiority of capitalism over slavery in 'Results of the Immediate Process of Production', ibid., pp. 1031–4.
19 Sen, *Development as Freedom*, p. 27.
20 K. Polanyi, *The Great Transformation* (Boston, 1957), p. 60; see generally ibid., chs 4 and 5.
21 Ibid., pp. 68–9. Polanyi's definition of a market economy bears a close resemblance to Marx's concept of generalized commodity production: see *Capital*, I, Parts 1 and 2.
22 Polanyi, *Great Transformation*, pp. 132, 134, 135; see also ibid., chs 6, 7, 12.
23 Callinicos, *Equality*, pp. 64–79, and, for example, F. A. Hayek, *The Fatal Conceit* (London, 1988), pp. 117–19.
24 See also Bellamy Foster, *Vulnerable Planet*, chs 6 and 7, and *Contre Temps*, 4 (2002).
25 For example, A. Nove, *The Economics of Feasible Socialism* (London, 1983), and R. Blackburn, 'After the Crash', *New Left Review*, (I) 185 (1991).
26 For example, D. Miller, *Market, State and Community* (Oxford, 1989), and J. Roemer, *A Future for Socialism* (London, 1994).
27 It is for this reason that G. A. Cohen regards market socialism as a second-best solution compared to a fully socialist society that he no longer believes to be feasible: see, for example, *Self-Ownership, Freedom, and Equality* (Cambridge, 1995), ch. 11.
28 Moreover, as Fikret Adaman and Pat Devine point out in their valuable critical survey of the debates on socialism and the market since the 1920s, market socialist models tend to accept the neo-classical assumption that economic actors have perfect information that has been so effectively criticized by Hayek and the 'Austrian' school: 'On the Economic Theory of Socialism', *New Left Review*, (I) 221 (1997), pp. 64–73.

29 W. Hutton, *The State We're In* (London, 1995), and *The World We're In* (London, 2002).

30 Polanyi, *Great Transformation*, p. 251.

31 John Grahl offers a pessimistic view of Germany's and Japan's capacity to resist these pressures: see 'Globalized Finance', *New Left Review*, (II) 8 (2001), pp. 41–7.

32 P. Gowan, L. Panitch, and M. Shaw, 'The State, Globalization and the New Imperialism: A Roundtable Discussion', *Historical Materialism*, 9 (2001), p. 15.

33 Yu Yongding, 'China: The Case for Capital Controls', in W. Bello et al., eds, *Global Finance* (London, 2000).

34 For the role played by the 'permanent arms economy' in post-war capitalism, see C. Harman, *Explaining the Crisis* (London, 1984), ch. 3.

35 Luc Boltanski and Eve Chapiello present in *Le Nouvel esprit du capitalisme* (Paris, 1999) just such a cyclical interpretation of the history of capitalism in which the prevailing capitalist 'spirit' generates a critique that leads to its correction and reform in a new 'spirit' till that too is undermined by yet another critique, and so on.

36 I say 'in general' because modern societies typically require individuals to work for others some of the time (for example, by requiring them to pay income tax) – though the rich are usually able to evade a proportionate share of this burden. Moreover, *in extremis* societies assume the right to conscript labour, as, for example, the British Parliament did when, as the fall of France to Hitler's armies became imminent, it passed in the space of a day (22 May 1940), an Emergency Powers Act that 'gave the government practically unlimited authority over all British citizens and their property', A. J. P. Taylor, *English History 1914–1945* (Harmondsworth, 1970), p. 583.

37 Bill Jordan has taxed me for failing, in an earlier book (*Equality*) to take into account the fact that economic globalization has greatly strengthened 'exit' – withdrawal from a deteriorating situation – as opposed to 'voice' – collective action to improve the situation (for this distinction, see A. O. Hirschmann, *Exit, Voice, and Loyalty*, Cambridge MA, 1970). 'Since 1989 . . . ,' Jordan writes, 'mobility is the key to advantage,' 'Liberal Egalitarianism and Marxist Critical Theory', *Imprints*, 6:1 (2002), p. 74. The privileged –

not just capitalists but also those with scarce skills – can use their right to exit much more effectively than the poor, who are 'stuck in "communities of fate" '. I advocate 'a return to a world in which privileged exit rights would be blocked, and popular voice rights made more fully effective', where a more appropriate response would be to give 'the subordinate and the vulnerable' stronger exit rights in the form of a basic income that 'would give workers an alternative to wage labour' and thus 'a relevant counter to the power of capital to move elsewhere', ibid., pp. 76, 77, 78. But, as Jordan concedes, to be effective basic income would have to be introduced internationally, since a country that made this reform on its own would be vulnerable to large-scale exit in the form of capital flight. In this respect, basic income is no different from a planned socialist economy. It is not clear how Jordan can help himself to the consideration that privileged exit can be countered only at the international level while implicitly denying this to socialist planning. This criticism (developed further in *Equality*, pp. 114–18) does not mean I oppose the idea of a universal basic income, as the next section makes clear.

38 F. A. von Hayek [1937], 'Economics and Knowledge', in *Individualism and the Economic Order* (London, 1949), and 'Competition as a Discovery Procedure', in idem, *New Studies in Philosophy, Politics, Economics and the History of Ideas* (London, 1978).

39 Boltanski and Chapiello, *Le Nouvel esprit du capitalisme*, offer the most exhaustive analysis of conceptualizations of contemporary capitalism as a network.

40 See A. Callinicos, *The Revenge of History* (Cambridge, 1991), esp. ch. 2.

41 P. Devine, *Democracy and Economic Planning* (Cambridge, 1988), pp. 109–10.

42 Ibid., p. 189

43 Devine imagines a single planning commission drafting the plan variants, but there seems to be no reason why there should not be several planning commissions each given the resources to draft and present alternative plans.

44 Ibid., pp. 191, 248; see generally ibid., Part IV.

45 Ibid., pp. 253, 265–6.

46 Ibid., p. 210. Devine argues that negotiated coordination 'differs fundamentally from the classical Marxist view' that communism brings the end of politics. For a different interpretation of classical Marxism and of communism, see Callinicos, *Revenge of History*, ch. 4.

47 F. Chesnais et al. [2000], 'L'Avenir du "movement anti-mondialiste": quelques premières réflexions en vue d'une consolidation théorique' (text circulated by e-mail), p. 6. Boris Kagarlitsky has an interesting discussion of property-forms in *The Twilight of Globalization* (London, 2000), ch. 2.

48 T. Cliff, 'Marxism and the Collectivization of Agriculture', *International Socialism*, (1) 19 (1964–5). The most important contemporary rural movement, the MST in Brazil, illustrates the complexity of the agrarian question today: see S. Branford and J. Rocha, *Cutting the Wire* (London, 2002).

49 Chesnais et al., 'L'Avenir du "movement anti-mondialiste"', p. 7.

50 Daniel Bensaïd emphasizes the democratic character of any alternative to capitalism in *Le Sourire du spectre: nouvel esprit du communisme* (Paris, 2000).

51 N. Klein, *No Logo* (London, 2000), p. 428.

52 C. Hines, *Localization: A Global Manifesto* (London, 2000).

53 M. Barratt Brown, extract in D. Ransom, *The No-Nonsense Guide to Fair Trade* (London, 2001), pp. 130–1.

54 B. Jetin and S. de Brunhoff, 'The Tobin Tax and the Regulation of Capital Movements', in Bello et al., eds, *Global Finance*, p. 201.

55 For a series of British case-studies illustrating this claim, see G. Monbiot, *Captive State* (London, 2000).

56 M. Husson, *Le Grand bluff capitaliste* (Paris, 2001), Part II, ch. 2.

57 N. Ferguson, *The Cash Nexus* (London, 2001), pp. 310–11.

58 For a more cautious version of the case made here, see M. Dummett, *On Immigration and Refugees* (London, 2001).

59 Available from www.unep.org.

60 *Financial Times*, 18 February 2002.

61 C. Serfati, *La Mondialisation armée* (Paris, 2001), p. 161.

62 *Financial Times*, 27 February 2002.

63 For an example of such a programme see [1934] 'A Programme of Action for France', in L. D. Trotsky, *Writings 1934–35* (New York, 1974), pp. 20–32.

Afterword

1 W. B. Gallie, *Philosophy and the Historical Understanding* (London, 1964), ch. 8.
2 I owe this insight to Sam Ashman.
3 D. Held, A. McGrew et al., *Global Transformations* (Cambridge, 1999). For further critical discussion of the globalization debate, see A. Callinicos, *Against the Third Way* (Cambridge, 2001), ch. 1.
4 C. Harman, 'Globalization: A Critique of a New Orthodoxy', *International Socialism*, (2) 73 (1996); P. Hirst and G. Thompson, *Globalization in Question* (Cambridge, 1996); R. Gilpin, *The Challenge of Global Capitalism* (Princeton, 2000); and N. Ferguson, *The Cash Nexus* (London, 2001).
5 H. James, *The End of Globalization* (Cambridge MA, 2001), pp. 2, 224. Meghnad Desai in *Marx's Revenge* (London, 2002) similarly portrays the history of capitalism over the past 150 years as that of two great waves of globalization at the end of the nineteenth and twentieth centuries punctuated by the disintegration of the world market into national capitalisms between 1914 and the 1970s.
6 James, *End of Globalization*, p. 223.
7 D. Bensaïd [2002], 'Le Nouvel internationalisme', due to appear in the *Encyclopaedia Universalis*. For a synoptic historical overview, see P. Anderson, 'Internationalism: A Breviary', *New Left Review*, (II) 14 (2002).
8 Bensaïd', 'Le Nouvel internationalisme'.
9 *Financial Times*, 30 November 2001.
10 'President to Send Secretary Powell to Middle East', 4 April 2002, www.whitehouse.gov.
11 The historical and philosophical issues implied by this argument are explored at length in A. Callinicos, *Equality* (Cambridge, 2000). Jacques Derrida offers a critique of fraternity that is at once stimulating and infuriating in *Politics of Friendship* (London, 1997).

Index